Private Papers Of William Wilberforce

William Wilberforce

Nabu Public Domain Reprints:

You are holding a reproduction of an original work published before 1923 that is in the public domain in the United States of America, and possibly other countries. You may freely copy and distribute this work as no entity (individual or corporate) has a copyright on the body of the work. This book may contain prior copyright references, and library stamps (as most of these works were scanned from library copies). These have been scanned and retained as part of the historical artifact.

This book may have occasional imperfections such as missing or blurred pages, poor pictures, errant marks, etc. that were either part of the original artifact, or were introduced by the scanning process. We believe this work is culturally important, and despite the imperfections, have elected to bring it back into print as part of our continuing commitment to the preservation of printed works worldwide. We appreciate your understanding of the imperfections in the preservation process, and hope you enjoy this valuable book.

Private Papers Of William Wilberforce

William Wilberforce

Nabu Public Domain Reprints:

You are holding a reproduction of an original work published before 1923 that is in the public domain in the United States of America, and possibly other countries. You may freely copy and distribute this work as no entity (individual or corporate) has a copyright on the body of the work. This book may contain prior copyright references, and library stamps (as most of these works were scanned from library copies). These have been scanned and retained as part of the historical artifact.

This book may have occasional imperfections such as missing or blurred pages, poor pictures, errant marks, etc. that were either part of the original artifact, or were introduced by the scanning process. We believe this work is culturally important, and despite the imperfections, have elected to bring it back into print as part of our continuing commitment to the preservation of printed works worldwide. We appreciate your understanding of the imperfections in the preservation process, and hope you enjoy this valuable book.

WILLIAM WILBERFORCE, M.P
FOR THE COUNTY OF YORK.

Private Papers
of
William Wilberforce

*Collected and Edited, with a
Preface, by A. M. Wilberforce*

With Portraits

London
T. FISHER UNWIN
1897

[All rights reserved.]

PREFACE

WILLIAM WILBERFORCE is remembered on account of his long and successful efforts for the Abolition of the Slave Trade. In a House of Commons that counted Pitt, Fox, Burke, and Sheridan amongst its members, he held a front rank both as a speaker and debater. Of one of his speeches in 1789 Burke said, "it equalled anything he had heard in modern times, and was not, perhaps, to be surpassed in the remains of Grecian eloquence." And Pitt said, "Of all the men I ever knew Wilberforce has the greatest natural eloquence." But an even greater power than his oratory was perhaps the influence that he acquired over all ranks of society. Friendship is often the means by which influence is gained, and Wilberforce's friendship with Pitt, beginning long before his anti-Slave Trade days and continued till the end of Pitt's life, was no doubt the source of a strong personal influence.

It has been said that nothing in history is more creditable and interesting than Pitt's long and brotherly intimacy with Wilberforce, widely as they differed in their views of life.

To give an idea of the terms of their friendship these letters, possibly mislaid by the biographers of Wilberforce, from Pitt to Wilberforce are now published.[1]

Lord Rosebery thought the letters "among the most interesting we possess of Pitt," and we gladly acceded to his wish to print a few copies privately.

The Rev. W. F. Wilberforce has kindly consented to the publication of the matured estimate of Pitt's character mentioned in the "Life of Wilberforce," with an intimation that "it might hereafter appear in a separate form."

Other letters from some of the most distinguished men of the time show the many and varied interests of Wilberforce's life, and seem to us too valuable to remain hidden in obscurity.

The home letters published are from Wilber-

[1] All Pitt's letters are carefully preserved in the library of Lavington House with the exception of this series which was found in a disused cupboard.

force to his daughter Elizabeth, and to his son Samuel, afterwards Bishop of Oxford and Winchester. The letters to the latter are from the collection of 600 letters written by the father to the son.

A. M. WILBERFORCE.

LAVINGTON, *September* 1, 1897.

CONTENTS

	PAGE
LETTERS FROM PITT	1
SKETCH OF PITT BY W. WILBERFORCE	43
LETTERS FROM FRIENDS	83
HOME LETTERS	163

ILLUSTRATIONS

PAGE

1. WILLIAM WILBERFORCE, M.P. FOR THE COUNTY OF YORK . . . . *Frontispiece.*
   (*From a picture by J. Rising.*)

2. WILBERFORCE OAK . . . *Facing page* 17
   (At the foot of an old tree at Hollwood, after a conversation with Pitt, Wilberforce resolved to give notice in the House of Commons of his intention to bring forward the Abolition of the Slave Trade.)

3. THE RIGHT HONOURABLE WILLIAM PITT
   Facing page 79
   (*From a plate taken from an original drawing by the late Mr. Sayers.*)

4. BIRTHPLACE OF WILLIAM WILBERFORCE AT HULL . . . . *Facing page* 163

5. SAMUEL WILBERFORCE, AGED 29 ,, 245
   (*From a drawing by George Richmond.*)

LETTERS FROM PITT

LETTERS FROM PITT.

THE first of Pitt's letters to Wilberforce is "perhaps the only one extant that is racy of those rollicking times when the 'fruits of Pitt's earlier rising' appeared in the careful sowing of the garden beds with the fragments of Ryder's opera hat."[1]

"GRAFTON STREET,
"<i>July</i> 31, 1782.

"DEAR WILBERFORCE,—I shall not have the least difficulty in applying immediately to Lord Shelburne in behalf of your friend Mr. Thompson, and the favour is not such as to require a great exertion of interest, if there has been no prior engagement. I will let you know the result as soon as I can. Pray have no delicacy in mentioning to me whatever occurs of any kind in which I can be of any use to you. Whenever there is anything to prevent my doing as I should wish in consequence, I will tell you, so we shall be upon fair terms. I trust you

---

[1] Lord Rosebery's preface to "Pitt and Wilberforce Letters,' privately printed.

find all possible advantage from sea-bathing and sea-air. . . . I am as well as it is possible in the midst of all this *sin and sea coal*, and, for a Chancellor of the Exchequer who has exchanged his *happier hour*, pass my time very tolerably. Even Goostree's is not absolutely extinct, but has a chance of living thro' the dog days. I shall be happy to hear from you, whether in the shape of an official despatch or a familiar epistle. I am very glad to see you write without the assistance of a secretary. Perhaps, however, you will not be able to read without the assistance of a decypherer. At least in compassion to your eyesight it is as well for me to try it no further.

"So adieu. Yrs. ever sincerely,

"W. PITT."

"BRIGHTHELMSTONE,
"*Wednesday, Aug. 6, 1783.*

"DEAR WILBERFORCE,—*Anderson's Dictionary* I have received, and am much obliged to you for it. I will return it safe, I hope not dirtied, and possibly not read. I am sorry that you give so bad an account of your eyes, especially as this very letter looks as if it would put them to a severe trial, and might even defy the decypherer St. John, almost without the help of an ænigma. I have only to tell you that I have *no news*, which I consider as making it pretty certain that there will be none now before the meeting of Parliament. The party to Rheims hold of course, at least as far as depends upon me; which is at least one good effect certain. I wrote yesterday to Eliot,[1] apprising him, that I should be ready to meet him at Bankes's[2] before the last day of August; that I conceived we must proceed from thence to London, and that we ought to start within the three or four first days of September. I hope you will bear all these things in mind, and recollect that you have to do with punctual men, who would not risk their characters by being an hour too late for any appointment. The lounge here is excellent, principally owing to our keeping very much to ourselves—that is Pulchritudo, Steele, Pretyman, and myself. The Woodlys have been here in high foining, and have talked me to death. I would not bind myself to be a listener for life for a good deal. Your friend the Commodore treated us with his company at one or two assemblies, but was called back to defend some prizes, which there are those who contest with him, and which I fancy he thinks *the greatest instance of malignity he ever knew.* Mrs. Johnstone and Mrs. Walpole are left to dispute the prize here. The first is clearly the handsomer woman, but the husband of the latter looks the quieter man, and the better part of

[1] Hon. Edward James Eliot, brother-in-law of Pitt.
[2] Mr. Henry Bankes, Wilberforce's life-long friend.

love as well as valor is discretion. I conclude as you did, by desiring you to write immediately. I go from hence to Somersetshire this day sennight, and stay till Bankes's. Direct to Burton Pynsent, Somerset, and *if you will*, by London.

"Ever sincerely yrs.,

"W. Pitt."

Pitt's next letter refers to the General Election of 1784, and William Wilberforce's candidature for Yorkshire, which county he represented in Parliament for twenty-eight years.

"Downing Street,
"*Tuesday, April* 6, 1784.

"Dear Wilberforce,—I have received your two expresses, and one this morning from Mr. Wyvill. I could not get to town till late last night, but sent forward the letters you desired, and have done all I can on the several subjects you mention.

"I have applied to our friends in town to pay in the subscriptions, and I hope it will be done speedily. I inquired at Cambridge with regard to the different colleges. Trinity and St. John's have, I believe, as might be expected, the most interest, and will both exert it for you. Christ's has some, and I left that in a good train. I have spoken to Lord Temple, which is the only channel that has yet occurred to me about Oxford, who thinks he can be of use there. Wesley I have no doubt may be secured, and I will lose no time in seeing him if necessary, which I shall not think *at all awkward* at such a time. Steps are taking to procure a meeting of freeholders in your and Duncombe's interest, which I hope will answer. I have sent to Robinson and Hamilton. Lady Downe has been applied to, but can be brought to nothing more than perfect neutrality. Nesbitt's interest is secured, and he is thoroughly zealous. I do not well know how to get at his Grace of York, but will try every way I can. Lord Percy, I am afraid, cannot be brought to subscribe, tho' I do not quite despair of it. His objection seems now from some delicacy towards Weddell, with whom he has been much connected. He has, however, written to exert all his interest in your cause—particularly to Major Pallerne and Mr. Rayne, whom Mr. Wyvill mentions in his last letter. Lord Grantham, as I wrote you word before, must go with Weddell. I expect to hear something more of Lord Hawke, but I know he is now in the best disposition. I shall keep my messenger an hour or two to send the account of to-day's poll in Westminster, yesterday and to-day having been considered as the great push. Pray send me as quick an account as possible, and continue it from time to time, if a poll goes on. I hope you will be ready with a candidate at Hull on the supposition of your being seated for Yorkshire, which I am sanguine enough hardly to doubt. We are more successful everywhere, with only a very few exceptions, than can be imagined. I hope you bear all the fatigue tolerably. I wish it was over. God bless you.

"Most truly yours,

"W. PITT.

"Compts. to Smith, and many thanks for his letter. I hope he is still with you. The numbers at Westminster to-day are—

Hood.	Wray.	Fox.
3936	3622	3413

Sawbridge has beat Atkinson only by seven, and there is to be a scrutiny. The other members are Watson, Lewes, and Newnham. Sir R. Clayton declines for Surrey. Byng will probably be beat."

"DOWNING STREET,

"*Sunday, December* 19, 1784.

"MY DEAR WILBERFORCE,—I have been so diligently *turning my thoughts* on all sides since we parted, that tho' they have been turned to you as often as to any other quarter, I have never found the moment to put them into writing till now. I have not time to thank you sufficiently for the picturesque and poetical epistle I received from you dated, as I remember, from your boat, from the inside and the imperial of your postchaise, and two or three places more, and containing among a variety of accurate descriptions one in particular, viewed from all those different situations, of the sun setting in the middle of the day. I hope the whole of your tour has continued to be embellished by these happy incidents, and has kept you throughout in as mad and rhapsodical a mood as at that moment. I have some remorse in the immediate occasion of my writing to you just now; which, however, all things considered, I am bound to overcome. Be it known to you, then, that as much as I wish you to bask on, under an Italian sun, I am perhaps likely to be the instrument of snatching you from your present paradise, and hurrying you back to 'the rank vapours of this sin-worn mould.' A variety of circumstances concur to make it necessary to give notice immediately on the meeting of Parliament of the day on which I shall move the question of the Reform. We meet on the *25th of January*, and I think *about three weeks after*, which will allow full time for a call of the House, will be as late as I can easily defer it. I would not for a thousand reasons have you absent, tho' I hate that you should come before your time, and if any particular circumstances made a week or ten days a matter of real importance to you, I think I could postpone it as long as that.

"Only let me hear from you positively before the meeting of Parliament. The chief thing necessary is that I should then be able to name *some* day, and the precise day is of less consequence. You will hardly believe me if I tell you that I entertain the strongest hope of coming very near, if not absolutely succeeding. I have seen the Oracle of Yorkshire, Wyvill, and made him compleatly happy with the prospect.

"All things are going, on the whole, exceeding well. You will have learnt that the *Old Boy* at last overcame his doubts, and has ventured single into the Cabinet, which is a great point happily settled. God bless you.

"Ever most faithfully yours.

"W. PITT."

"1784.

"MY DEAR WILBERFORCE,—I am sorry to find from your letter from Nottingham that the Knight of Yorkshire is in so much dudgeon. Tho', to say the truth, the instances of neglect you mention are enough to provoke common patience. What is worse, I know no remedy for it. My letter, which missed you, contained no other information than that the place of Marshall of the Admiralty had been long since filled up. Some of the world is here at present, and will be multiplying every day till the meeting of Parliament. I expect Eliot in a very few days. I know nothing of Bankes very lately. Pray come to Wimbledon as soon as possible; I want to talk with you about your navy bills, which, tho' all your ideas now must go to landed property, you should not entirely forget, and about ten thousand other things. By the by, Lord Scarborough is risen from the dead, as you probably know. I have just received an account from Whitbread that St. Andrew loses his election by three; and would probably lose by more if he chooses a scrutiny or a petition. Adieu.

"Ever yrs.,
"W. PITT.

"For the sake of this letter I am leaving a thousand others unanswered, and a thousand projects unread. You will probably think it was hardly worth while."

The brotherly intimacy between Pitt and Wilberforce is clearly shown in the next letter. Wilberforce had written to Pitt to tell him of the change in his religious opinions, and, in consequence, of his probable retirement from political life. He no doubt thought that Pitt would fail to sympathise with his altered views, but the man who was "so absorbed in politics that he had never given himself time for due reflection on religion"[1] wished to understand the religious difficulties of his friend, and with the greatest tenderness begs him to open

[1] "Life of Wilberforce," vol. i. p. 95.

his mind to "one who does not know how to separate your happiness from his own."

"Downing Street,
"*December* 2, 1785.

"My dear Wilberforce,—Bob Smith [1] mentioned to me on Wednesday the letters he had received from you, which prepared me for that I received from you yesterday. I am indeed too deeply interested in whatever concerns you not to be very sensibly affected by what has the appearance of a new æra in your life, and so important in its consequences for yourself and your friends. As to any public conduct which your opinions may ever lead you to, I will not disguise to you that few things could go nearer my heart than to find myself differing from you essentially on any great principle.

"I trust and believe that it is a circumstance which can hardly occur. But if it ever should, and even if I should experience as much pain in such an event, as I have found hitherto encouragement and pleasure in the reverse, believe me it is impossible that it should shake the sentiments of affection and friendship which I bear towards you, and which I must be forgetful and insensible indeed if I ever could part with. They are sentiments engraved in my heart, and will never be effaced or weakened.

[1] Afterwards first Lord Carrington.

If I knew how to state all I feel, and could hope that you are open to consider it, I should say a great deal more on the subject of the resolution you seem to have formed. You will not suspect me of thinking lightly of any moral or religious motives which guide you. As little will you believe that I think your understanding or judgment easily misled. But forgive me if I cannot help expressing my fear that you are nevertheless deluding yourself into principles which have but too much tendency to counteract your own object, and to render your virtues and your talents useless both to yourself and mankind. I am not, however, without hopes that my anxiety paints this too strongly. For you confess that the character of religion is not a gloomy one, and that it is not that of an enthusiast. But why then this preparation of solitude, which can hardly avoid tincturing the mind either with melancholy or superstition? If a Christian may act in the several relations of life, must he seclude himself from them all to become so? Surely the principles as well as the practice of Christianity are simple, and lead not to meditation only but to action. I will not, however, enlarge upon these subjects now. What I would ask of you, as a mark both of your friendship and of the candour which belongs to your mind, is to open yourself fully and without reserve to one, who, believe me, does not know how to separate your happiness from his own. You do not explain either the degree or the duration of the retirement which you have prescribed to yourself; you do not tell me how the future course of your life is to be directed, when you think the same privacy no longer necessary; nor, in short, what idea you have formed of the duties which you are from this time to practise. I am sure you will not wonder if I am inquisitive on such a subject. The only way in which you can satisfy me is by conversation. There ought to be no awkwardness or embarrassment to either of us, tho' there may be some anxiety; and if you will open to me fairly the whole state of your mind on these subjects, tho' I shall venture to state to you fairly the points where I fear we may differ, and to desire you to re-examine your own ideas where I think you are mistaken, I will not importune you with fruitless discussion on any opinion which you have deliberately formed. You will, I am sure, do justice to the motives and feelings which induce me to urge this so strongly to you. I think you will not refuse it; if you do not, name any hour at which I can call upon you to-morrow. I am going into Kent, and can take Wimbledon in my way. Reflect, I beg of you, that no principles are the worse for being discussed, and believe me that at all events the full knowledge of the nature and extent of your opinions and intentions will be to me a lasting satisfaction.

"Believe me, affectionately and unalterably yours,

"W. PITT."

Pitt came the next morning according to his proposal in this remarkable letter: when Wilberforce [1] "conversed with Pitt near two hours, and opened myself completely to him.... He tried to reason me out of my convictions, but soon found himself unable to combat their correctness if Christianity were true." To quote Lord Rosebery's Preface [2] to these letters: "Surely a memorable episode, this heart-searching of the young saint and the young minister. They went their different ways, each following their high ideal in the way that seemed best to him. And so it went on to the end, Wilberforce ever hoping to renew the sacred conversation."

"DOWNING STREET,
"*September*, 23, 1786.

"MY DEAR WILBERFORCE,—At length all the obstacles of business, of idleness, and of procrastination are so far overcome that I find myself with my pen in my hand to answer your three letters. I have seriously had it upon my conscience for

---

[1] "Life of Wilberforce," vol. i. p. 95.
[2] Privately printed.

some time; but yet I believe it is another influence to which this present writing is to be immediately ascribed. Having yesterday parted with the ornament on my cheek, and two or three handkerchiefs for the present occupying the place of it, my appearance is better suited to correspondence than conversation; and in addition to this I happen to have an interval freer from business than at any time since Parliament rose. Our French Treaty is probably by this time actually signed, or will at most not require more than one more messenger to settle everything; but the winds have been so unfavourable that I have been, for some days longer than I expected, in suspense as to the issue of it. Two or three more treaties are on the anvil, and I think we shall meet with the appearance of not having spent an idle or (as I flatter myself) a fruitless summer. The multitude of things depending has made the Penitentiary House long in deciding upon. But I still think a beginning will be made in it before the season for building is over; and if its progress is as quick as that of my room at Hollwood, bolts and bars will be useless before another season. I am very glad you like our new Board of Trade, which I have long felt to be one of the most necessary, and will be now one of the most efficient departments of Government. The colony for Botany Bay will be much indebted to you for your assist-

WILBERFORCE OAK.

ance in providing a chaplain. The enclosed will, however, show you that its interests have not been neglected, as well as that you have a nearer connection with them than perhaps you were yourself aware of. Seriously speaking, if you can find such a clergyman as you mention we shall be very glad of it; but it must be soon. My sister was brought to bed of a daughter on Wednesday, and was at first surprising well; but she has since had some fever, which was to such a degree yesterday as to make us very uneasy. She is now, however, almost entirely free from it, and going on as well as possible. I am in hopes of getting into Somersetshire the middle of next week for about ten days. Soon after I hope I may see you at Hollwood. Bob Smith was in town lately, much better on the whole, but not quite so well as I hoped to see him. Adieu.

"Ever yours,

"W. Pitt."

"Downing Street,
"*Tuesday, April* 8, 1788.

"My dear Wilberforce,—I have just received your letter of yesterday, and as I can easily imagine how much the subject of it interests you, I will not lose a moment in answering it. As to the Slave Trade, I wish on every account it should come forward in your hands rather than any other. But that in the present year is impracticable; and I only hope you will resolve to dismiss it as much as possible from your mind. It is both the rightest and wisest thing you can do. If it will contribute to setting you at ease, that *I* should personally bring it forward (supposing circumstances will admit of its being brought forward this session) your wish will decide. At all events, if it is in such a state that it can be brought on, I will take care that it shall be moved in a respectable way, and I will take my part in it as actively as if I was myself the mover. And if I was to consult entirely my own inclination or opinion, I am not sure whether this may not be best for the business itself; but on this, as I have said already, your wish shall decide me. With regard to the possibility of its being brought on and finished this session, I can hardly yet judge. The inquiry has been constantly going on, and we have made a great progress. But it takes unavoidably more time than I expected. In one word, however, be assured that I will continue to give the business constant attention, and do everything to forward it. Whenever it is in such a state that you could yourself have brought it on with advantage to the cause, I will do it or undertake for its being done, in whatever way seems most proper. I mean, therefore, to accept it as a trust from you to the whole extent you can wish, and to make myself responsible for it, unless it is necessarily delayed till you are able to resume it yourself.

"Any applications from your Society shall most certainly be attended to. Justice Addington's grievance in particular, which I was before acquainted with by a memorial, will be immediately removed. I do not like to write you a longer letter than is absolutely necessary. I trust I need not lengthen it to tell how impatiently I look to the satisfaction of seeing you again, as stout and strong as I hope you will return to us. Let me have from time to time a line from any hand you can most conveniently employ, to tell me how you go on, and what are your motions during the summer. I wish I may be able to arrange mine, when holidays come, so as to fall in with you somewhere or other. As soon as I can judge about Parliament meeting before Christmas or not, you shall hear. If it sits pretty late now, it probably will not meet till after. Adieu for the present. Every good wish attend you.

"Ever affectionately yours,
"W. PITT."

I have had very good accounts of you from two or three quarters.

"PEMBROKE HALL,
"*Saturday, June* 28, 1788.

"MY DEAR WILBERFORCE,—I have no small

pleasure in writing to you quietly from hence, after hearing the good account you sent me of yourself confirmed by those who saw you then, and especially by our friend Glynn. I am lucky enough to have a wet evening, which, besides the good I hope it will do to the country at large, has the peculiar advantage of preventing me from paying my personal respects to any one of my constituents, and so gives me the leisure to answer *seriatim* the several sections of your letter. The business respecting the Slave Trade meets just now with some rub in the House of Lords, even in the temporary regulation respecting the conveyance, which I wonder how any human being can resist, and which I therefore believe we shall carry; tho' it creates some trouble, and will still protract the session a week or ten days. We hear very little yet from the West Indies, but a few weeks must bring more, and I have no doubt the summer may be employed in treating with foreign Powers to advantage. I shall set about it with the utmost activity and with good hopes of success, tho' founded as yet rather on general grounds than any positive information. There seems not a shadow of doubt as to the conduct of the House of Commons next year, and I think with good management the difficulties in the other House may be got over. Your plan of a mission to Bengal I mention only to show the punctuality of answering your letter, as you reserve the discussion till we meet. As for Dr. Glass, I was obliged to answer Thornton, who applied to me for some such person (I think for this same Dr. Glass), that the state of my engagements leaves me not at liberty at present, and if you have any occasion to say anything about it to them, be so good to speak of it in the same style. Of the Penitentiary Houses what can I say more? But in due time they shall not be forgotten.

"My plan of visiting you and your lakes is, I assure you, not at all laid aside. I cannot speak quite certainly as to the time, but if there happens nothing which I do not now foresee, it will be either the beginning or middle of August; I rather think the former, but I shall be able to judge better in about a fortnight, and then you shall hear from me. Nothing is decided about the meeting of Parliament, but it is clear the trial will not go on till February. I rather believe, however, that we ought to meet and employ a month before Christmas; as what with Slave Trade, Quebec Petition, Poor Laws, Tobacco, &c., we shall have more on our hands than can be got through in any decent time while we are exposed to the interruption from Westminster Hall. I think I have now dispatched all the points to which I was called upon to reply, and come now to open my own budget; which must be done, however, in a *whisper*, and must not as yet be repeated even to the most solitary echoes of Windermere. You will wonder what mystery I have to impart. At the first part you will not be much surprised, which is that Lord Howe and his friend Brett are to quit the Admiralty as soon as the session closes. The cause (tho' its effects have slept so long) is what passed last summer respecting the promotion of Sir Charles Middleton. You will not come to the surprising part when I add that Lord Howe's successor must be a landman, as there is no seaman who is altogether fit for the first place at that board. But what will you say when I tell you that the landman in question is no other than my brother? He undertakes it very readily, and will I am sure set about the business in earnest, to which I believe you think him as equal as I do. Lord Hood is to be at the board; not without some risk of losing Westminster, but by keeping our secret till the moment, I hope even that may be saved; but it is comparatively of little consequence. I feel the arrangement is liable to some invidious objections, but I am satisfied they are more than counterbalanced by the solid advantage of establishing a compleat concert with so essential a department, and removing all appearance of a separate interest. I shall be impatient, however, to hear what you think of my scheme. There is nothing else that occurs worth adding to this long scrawl, and I am obliged to seal it up, as in spite of the rain which keeps me at home, I am in expectation of an agreeable collection of dons whom Turner has convened to smoke and sleep round his table this evening. God bless you.

"Believe me, ever affectionately yours,
"W. PITT.'

"DOWNING STREET,
"*Monday, September* 1, 1788.

"MY DEAR WILBERFORCE,—I have certainly given a considerable latitude to my promise of writing in a fortnight, in defence of which I have nothing to say, but that in addition to the common causes of delaying a letter I could not easily resolve to tell you that my northern scheme has for some time grown desperate. Powers farther north and the unsettled state of all the Continent (tho' not at all likely to involve us in anything disagreeable) require in our present system too much watching to allow for a long absence. I have not yet got even to Burton, which you will allow must be my first object. But I assure you I am not the more in love with Continental politics for having interfered with a prospect I had set my heart so much upon, as spending some quiet days on the bank of your lake. Pray let me know in your turn what your motions are likely to be, and when you think of being in this part of the world. Parliament will not meet till after Christmas. As to the Slave Trade, we are digesting our Report as far as present materials go, and you shall then have it; but we are still in expectation of the answer from the Islands. I had a long conversation with the French Ambassador on the subject some time ago, just before his going to France. He promised to represent it properly, and seemed to think there would be a favourable disposition. Their confusion has been such since that scarce anything was likely to be attended to; but I am in hopes Necker's coming in will prove very favourable to this object. The moment I hear anything respecting it I will write again; and at all events in less than *my last fortnight*. I must end now in haste to save the post and my dinner.

"Ever affectionately yours,
"W. PITT."

"DOWNING STREET,
"*Monday*, April 20, 1789.

"MY DEAR WILBERFORCE,—We have found it necessary to make some corrections on looking over the proof sheets of the Report, which will delay the presenting it till Wednesday. I shall have no difficulty in saying then that the business must of course be postponed on the grounds you mention, and I will move to fix it for this day fortnight if you see no objection. I imagine the House must meet on Friday on account of Hastings's business, but that will probably be a reason for their adjourning as soon as they come back from Westminster Hall, and your business may, I dare say, wait till Monday. In that case I would certainly meet you at Hollwood on Friday, as I wish extremely to talk over with you the whole business, and show you our project, with which, like most projectors, we are much delighted. From what you mention of the parts you have been studying, I do not imagine there is anything behind more material than what you have seen, but I see no part of our case that is not made out upon the strongest grounds. Steele has shown me your letter to him. There certainly cannot be the least reason for your coming up merely to attend St. Paul's.

"Ever affectionately yours,

"W. PITT."

"DOWNING STREET,
"*Wednesday, February* 2, 1796.

"MY DEAR WILBERFORCE,—I have seen Sir W. Fawcett, &c., and settled with them that they shall take *immediately* the necessary measures for having a sufficient number of officers to receive men at additional places of rendezvous. They propose for the West Riding (in addition to Pontefract), Bradford and Barnsley, as appearing to take in all the most material districts, and will send the orders accordingly; but any farther arrangement may be made afterwards which may appear to be wanting. This and the explanatory act will, I trust, quiet the difficulty. My cold is much better, and I have hardly any doubt of being in condition for service on Friday, to which day, you probably know, the business is put off. "Yours ever,

"W. P."

"Downing Street,
"*August* 4, 1796.

"My dear Wilberforce,—I am anxious not to let the post go without telling you that I cannot have a moment's hesitation in assuring you that in case of the Deanery of York becoming vacant, I shall with the utmost pleasure recommend Mr. Clarke to succeed to it. On the important points in your other letter, I have not time just now to write at large; but I think the idea you suggest very desirable to be carried into execution, and I will turn in my mind the means of putting it into train. I certainly am not inclined even now to think gloomily of public affairs; but I must at the same time own that I feel the crisis to be a most serious one, and to require the utmost exertion and management.

"Ever yours sincerely,
"W. Pitt."

"DOWNING STREET,
"*September* 7, 1796.

"MY DEAR WILBERFORCE,—I think it nearly certain that Parliament will meet on the 27th, and I wish much it may suit you to come this way some time before.

"Our application is gone for a passport for a person to go directly to Paris. The message of the Directory confessing in such strong terms their distress (and the Archduke's recent victory on the 22nd, the account of which is in last night's *Gazette*, may be relied on), give some chance that our overtures may be successful. In the meantime it will be indispensable to take very strong measures indeed, both of finance and military defence; and if the spirit of the country is equal to the exigency, I am confident all will yet end well. An immediate Spanish war is, I think, nearly certain. The only motive to it is the fear of France preponderating over their fear of us; and the pretexts as futile as could be wished. The alarm respecting the effect on our trade is greatly overrated, as the whole proportion of our exports thither compared with the rest of the world is inconsiderable. You will see that an Order of Council is published giving liberty for the export of manufactures and the payment of bills, which will, I hope, be satisfactory in your part of the world. I delayed writing to Mr. Cookson till I could tell him the measure was taken; and when it was taken, being in the hurry of a journey to Weymouth and back, I deferred it again, so that it was already announced in the *Gazette*, and it became too late to write. Perhaps you can make my excuses.

"Ever yours,

"W. P."

"DOWNING STREET,
"*September* 20, 1797.

"MY DEAR WILBERFORCE,—I know what your feelings will be on receiving the melancholy account which I have to send you, and which reached me from Cornwall this morning, that a renewal of Eliot's complaint has ended fatally and deprived us of him.

"After the attacks he has had, it is impossible to say that the blow could ever be wholly unexpected, but I had derived great hopes from the accounts for some time, and was not at this moment at all prepared for what has happened. You will not wonder that I cannot write to you on any other subject, but I will as soon as I can.

"Ever sincerely yours,

"W. PITT."

"*Friday*, 4 P.M.

"MY DEAR WILBERFORCE,—I am only anxious to avoid embarrassment to your question as well as to the general course of business; and will call on you in a few minutes on my way to the House.

"Ever aff. yours,

"W. P."

"DOWNING STREET,
"*Thursday, August* 14, 1800.

"MY DEAR WILBERFORCE,—I have no thoughts of going to Walmer till the very end of the month, and it is doubtful whether I can accomplish it then. In the interval the Castle is quite disengaged, and it will give me great pleasure if it can afford you any accommodation. If you should not find any situation before the 1st of September perfectly to your mind, I beg you to believe that your prolonging your stay will be no inconvenience and a great pleasure to me, supposing I am able to come. The improvements made since you were there, with the help of a cottage with some tolerable bedrooms, are quite sufficient for your family, and for myself and the only two or three persons who would be likely to come with me, such as perhaps Carrington, the Master of the Rolls, and Long. Be so good, therefore, to consult entirely your own convenience.

"Ever yours,

"W. P.

"Let me know what day next week you fix for being there, and everything shall be ready for you. You may as well send your servant to my manager

Bullock, who will arrange everything about cellar and other household concerns."

"PARK PLACE,
"October 1, 1801.

"MY DEAR WILBERFORCE,—I cannot refrain from congratulating you most sincerely on the happy event of the Signature of Preliminaries, which you will, I believe, hear from Addington. The terms are such as I am persuaded you will be well satisfied with, and tho' they are not in every point (particularly one material one) exactly all that I should have wished, I have no hesitation in saying that I think them on the whole highly honourable to the country and very advantageous. The event is most fortunate both for Government and the public, and for the sake of both, gives me infinite satisfaction. I am but just in time for the post.

"Ever sincerely yours,
"W. PITT."

"DOWNING STREET, *Saturday*.

"MY DEAR WILBERFORCE,—I shall be very glad if you can call here any time after nine this evening, as I wish to show you a paper from the other side of the water, of a very interesting nature, tho' not such as was most to be wished or at all to be expected. "Yours,
"W. P."

"WALMER CASTLE,
"*May* 31, 1802.

"MY DEAR WILBERFORCE,—I found your letter on my arrival here yesterday, having escaped to Hollwood on Friday only as a preparation for pursuing my journey hither with less interruption than I should have been exposed to, starting from town. An absence of ten days or a fortnight has been so much recommended, and indeed I began myself to feel so much in want of it, that I am afraid I must not think of returning for your motion. Indeed, tho' I should most eagerly support it (supposing you can provide, as I trust you can, means of making the execution in the detail practicable and effectual), I see no chance in the present state of the session of your carrying it, unless Addington can be brought really to see the propriety of it, and to concur in it at once without debate. This last I should hope might be managed, and whatever impression parts of his speech may have made on your mind, I am sure I need not suggest to you that the best chance of doing this will be to endeavour coolly to lay before him the case as it really is, unmixed as far as possible with any topics of soreness, which evidently were not absent from his mind on Canning's motion. I certainly, on the whole, judge much more favourably of his general intentions on the whole subject (or, I should rather say, of his probable conduct) than you do. But I admit that one part of his speech was as unsatisfactory as possible. This I really believe proceeded in a great measure from the evident embarrassment and distress under which he was speaking, and which I am persuaded prevented him from doing any justice to his own ideas. I may deceive and flatter myself, but tho' I know we shall be far from obtaining all that you and I wish, I really think there is much chance of great real and substantial ground being gained towards the ultimate and not remote object of total abolition next session. This is far from a reason for not endeavouring, if possible, to prevent the aggravation of the evil in the meantime, and I heartily wish you may be successful in the attempt.

"Ever affy. yrs.,

"W. P."

"WALMER CASTLE,
"*September* 22, 1802.

"MY DEAR WILBERFORCE,—I am much obliged to you for your kind letter of inquiry. My complaint has entirely left me. I am recovering my strength every day, and I have no doubt of being in a very short time as well as I was before the attack. Farquhar, however, seems strongly disposed to recommend Bath before the winter, and if you make your usual visit thither, I hope it is not impossible we may meet. Perhaps you will let me know whether you propose going before Parliament meets, and at what time. I hardly imagine that the session before Christmas can produce much business that will require attendance. I ought long since to have written to you on the subject of our friend Morritt. It would give me great pleasure to see him come back to Parliament, tho' I hardly think the occasion was one on which I

[Rest of letter torn off.]

"BATH,
  "October 31, 1802.

"MY DEAR WILBERFORCE,—As you are among the persons to whom the author of the enclosed high-flown compliments refers for his character for a very important purpose, I shall be much obliged to you if you will tell me what you know of him. A man's qualifications to give a dinner certainly depend more on the excellence of his cook and his wine, than on himself, but I have still some curiosity to know what sort of company he and his guests are likely to prove; and should therefore be glad to know a little more about them than I collect from his list of the *dramatis personæ*, which for instruction might as well have been taken from any old play-bill. In the meantime I have been obliged out of common civility, *provisoirement* to accept his invitation. I was very sorry that I had too little time to spare in passing thro' town to try to see you. I should have much wished to have talked over with you the events which have been passing and the consequences to which they seem to lead. You know how much under all the circumstances I wished for peace, and my wishes remain the same, if Bonaparte can be made to feel that he is not to trample in succession on every nation in Europe. But of this I fear there is little chance, and without it I see no prospect but war.

"I have not yet been here long enough to judge much of the effect of these waters, but as far as I can in a few days, I think I am likely to find them of material use to me. I mean to be in town by the 18th of next month. Paley's work, which you mentioned in your last letter, I had already read on the recommendation of my friend Sir W. Farquhar, who had met with it by accident, and was struck with its containing the most compendious and correct view of anatomy which he had ever seen. I do not mean that he thought this its only merit. It certainly has a great deal, but I think he carries some of his details and refinements further than is at all necessary for his purpose, and perhaps than will quite stand the test of examination.

"Ever affy. yrs.,

"W. P."

"WALMER CASTLE,
"*August* 8, 1803 (?).

"MY DEAR WILBERFORCE,—Not having returned from a visit to some of my corps on the Isle of Thanet till Friday evening, I could not answer your letter by that day's post, and I was interrupted when I was going to write to you yesterday. It was scarce possible for me, consistent with very material business in this district, to have reached town to-day; and besides, I confess, I do not think any great good could have been done by anything I could say in the House on any of the points you mention. I feel most of them, however, and some others of the same sort, as of most essential importance; and I have thoughts of coming to town for a couple of days (which is as much as I can spare from my duties here) towards the end of the week, to try whether I cannot find some channel by which a remedy may be suggested on some of the points which are now most defective. I think I shall probably reach town on Saturday morning, and I should wish much if you could contrive to meet me in Palace Yard or anywhere else, to have an hour's conversation with you. I will write to you again as soon as I can precisely fix any day. We are going on here most rapidly, and in proportion to our population, most extensively, in every species of local defence, both naval and military, and I trust shall both add very much to the security of essential points on this coast, and set not a bad example to other maritime districts.

"Ever affy. yours,
"W. P."

"Walmer Castle,
"*January* 5, 1804.

"My dear Wilberforce,—Your letter reached me very safe this morning, and I thank you very much for its contents. I hope it will not be long before I have an opportunity of talking over with you fully the subject to which it relates. From what I have heard since I saw you, it will be necessary for me pretty soon to make up my mind on the line to pursue under the new state of things which is approaching. In the meantime, I shall not commit myself to anything without looking to *all* the consequences as cautiously as you can wish; and before I form any final decision, I shall much wish to consult yourself and a few others whose opinions I most value. If no new circumstance arises to revive the expectation of the enemy, I mean to be in town the beginning of next week, and will immediately let you know. Perhaps I may be able to go on to Bath for a fortnight.

"Ever affy. yours,
"W. P."

Two examples are here given of Wilberforce's

letters to Pitt. The first is written in the character of a country member and political friend. The second is one in reference to his work on Practical Religion.[1] They are both, as is generally the case with his letters to Pitt, undated, but the post-mark of the second bears "1797."

Mr. Wilberforce to Right Hon. William Pitt.

"MY DEAR PITT,—My head and heart have been long full of some thoughts which I wished to state to you when a little less under extreme pressure than when Parliament is sitting. But my eyes have been very poorly. I am now extremely hurried, but I will mention two or three things as briefly as possible that I may not waste your time. First, perhaps even yet you may not have happened to see an Order in Council allowing, notwithstanding the War, an intercourse to subsist between our West Indian Colonies and those of Spain, in which negro slaves are the chief articles we are to supply. I know these commercial matters are not within your department, and that therefore your assent is asked, if at all, when your mind is full of other subjects. But let me only remind you, for it would be foolish to write what will suggest itself to your own mind, that the House of Commons did actually pass the

---

[1] "A Practical View of the Prevailing Religious System of Professed Christians," &c., London, 1797.

Bill for abolishing the foreign slave trade; and that if contracts are made again for supplying Spain for a term of years, it may throw obstacles in the way of a foreign slave-trade abolition. It would give me more pleasure than I can express to find any further measures, or even thoughts, on this to me painful subject, for many reasons, by hearing the order was revoked. Second, I promised by compulsion (I mean because I dislike to bore you) to state to you on the part of the Deputy Receiver General for the North and East Ridings of Yorkshire and Hull that it would tend materially both to facilitate and cheapen the collection of the new assessed taxes to let them be collected at the same time as the old ones. This will make the rounds four times per annum instead of ten, and he says the expense of collecting, if incurred six times per annum, will amount to full one-half of all the present salaries of the Receivers General in the Kingdom. As he is a most respectable man, I ought to say that he gives it as his opinion that the Receivers General are not overpaid, all things considered. But for my own opinion let me add that his principal really has none of the labours of the office, and the deputy even finds his securities for him. Third, surely there ought at the Bank to be a distinction between what is paid for assessed taxes and what as free donation, when the subscription includes both:

your own and those of many others are under that head. Fourth, I suppose you are now thinking of your taxes. Do, I beseech you, let one of them be a tax on all public diversions of every kind, including card-playing. I can't tell you how much their not being taxed has been mentioned with censure, and I promised to send you the enclosed letter from a very respectable man. I am sorry I did, but now have no option. But my first great object in writing to you is most earnestly to press on your attention a manuscript, which I have been desired to lay before you, relative to Naval Discipline. You must allow the writer to express himself with some perhaps unpleasant idea of self-importance. But he clearly foresaw the late Mutiny, and most strongly urged the adoption of preventive measures, which, had they been taken, I verily believe the greatest misfortune this country ever suffered would not have happened. That nothing was done is in my mind— But I need not run on upon this to me most painful topic, because it often suggests doubts whether I have not been myself to blame, who perused the scheme two years ago. Let me earnestly entreat you, my dear Pitt, to peruse it most seriously and impartially, and then let Dundas read it. If you judge it proper, then either send it Lord Spencer or to the writer, who is a good deal nettled at his former communications to Lord

Spencer not being attended to. I will send the manuscript by to-morrow's mail.

"Yours ever sincerely,
"W. W.

"Every one is calling out for you to summon the nation to arm itself in the common defence. You hear how nobly my Yorkshire men are acting. I must have more discussion on that head, for they still wish you to impose an equal rate on all property."

"BATH, *Easter Sunday*.

"MY DEAR PITT,—I am not unreasonable enough to ask you to read my book: but as it is more likely that when you are extremely busy than at any other time you may take it up for ten minutes, let me recommend it to you in that case to open on the last section of the fourth chapter, wherein you will see wherein the religion which I espouse differs practically from the common orthodox system. Also the sixth chapter has almost a right to a perusal, being the basis of all politics, and particularly addressed to such as you. At the same time I know you will scold me for introducing your name. May God bless you. This is the frequent prayer of your affectionate and faithful

"W. W."

[Postmarked 1797.]

Here ends the hitherto unpublished correspondence between Pitt and Wilberforce. On the occasion of Pitt's death, his brother, Lord Chatham, writes with regard to his funeral:

Lord Chatham to Mr. Wilberforce.
"DOVER STREET,
"*February* 15, 1806.

"I have many thanks to offer you for your very kind letter which I received this morning. Knowing, as I do, how truly the sentiments of friendship and affection you express, were returned on the part of my poor brother towards you, I can only assure you that it will afford me a most sensible gratification that you should have, as an old, intimate friend, some particular situation allotted to you in the last sad tribute to be paid to his memory. Believe me, with sincere regard, my dear sir,

"Yours very faithfully,

"CHATHAM."

Pitt was one of the few men whose lives have affected the destiny of nations. The actions of such men are so far-reaching, and the possibilities of the might-have-been so great, that history hardly ever passes a final verdict upon them. Wilberforce had unexampled opportunities of gauging the character and motives of Pitt, and certainly had no strong partisan bias to warp his judgment. His matured estimate of Pitt cannot fail therefore to be of peculiar interest. It was written in 1821, sixteen years after Pitt's death, and is printed exactly as Wilberforce left it. It will no doubt recall to the mind of the reader Scott's well-known lines:

> "With Palinure's undaunted mood,
>   Firm at his dangerous post he stood;
>   Each call for needful rest repelled
>   With dying hand the rudder held
>   Till, in his fall, with fateful sway
>   The steerage of the realm gave way!"[1]

---

[1] "Marmion," Introduction to Canto 1.

SKETCH OF PITT BY W. WILBERFORCE

SKETCH OF PITT BY W. WILBERFORCE.

CONSIDERING the effect of party spirit in producing a distrust of all that is said in favour of a public man by those who have supported him, and the equal measure of incredulity as to all that is stated of him by his opponents, it may not be without its use for the character of Mr. Pitt to be delineated by one who, though personally attached to him, was by no means one of his partisans; who even opposed him on some most important occasions, but who, always preserving an intimacy with him, had an opportunity of seeing him in all circumstances and situations, and of judging as much as any one could of his principles, dispositions, habits, and manners.

It seems indeed no more than the payment of a debt justly due to that great man that the friend who occasionally differed from him should prevent any mistake as to the grounds of those differences; and that as he can do it consistently with truth, he should aver, as in consistency with truth he can aver, that in every instance (with perhaps one exception only) in which his conscience prompted him to dissent from Mr. Pitt's *measures*, he nevertheless respected Mr. Pitt's *principles;* the differences arose commonly from a different view of facts, or a different estimate of contingencies and probabilities. Where there was a difference of political principles, it scarcely ever was such as arose from moral considerations; still less such as was produced by any distrust of Mr. Pitt's main intention being to promote the well-being and prosperity of his country.

Mr. Pitt from his early childhood had but an indifferent constitution; the gouty habit of body which harassed him throughout his life, was manifested by an actual fit of that disorder when he was still a boy. As early as fourteen years of age he was placed at Pembroke Hall, Cambridge; he had even then excited sanguine expectations of future eminence. His father had manifested a peculiar regard for him; he had never, I believe, been under any other than the paternal roof, where his studies had been superintended by a private tutor; and besides a considerable proficiency in the Greek and Latin languages, he had written a play in English, which was spoken of in high terms by those who had perused it. I am sorry to hear that this early fruit of genius is not anywhere to be found.

While he was at the University his studies, I understand, were carried on with steady diligence both in classics and mathematics, and though as a nobleman he could not establish his superiority over the other young men of his time by his place upon the tripos, I have been assured that his proficiency in every branch of study was such as would have placed him above almost all competitors. He continued at the University till he was near one-and-twenty, and it was during the latter part of that period that I became acquainted with him. I knew him, however, very little till the winter of 1779-80, when he occupied chambers in Lincoln's Inn, and I myself was a good deal in London. During that winter we became more acquainted with each other; we used often to meet in the Gallery of the House of Commons, and occasionally at Lady St. John's and at other places, and it was impossible not to be sensible of his extraordinary powers.

On the calling of a new Parliament in the beginning of September, 1780, I was elected one of the Members for Hull. Mr. Pitt, if I mistake not, was an unsuccessful candidate for the University of Cambridge; but about Christmas 1780-81, through the intervention of some common friends (more than one have claimed the honour of the first suggestion, Governor Johnston, the Duke of Rutland, &c.), he received and accepted an offer of a seat in Parliament made to him in the most handsome terms by Sir James Lowther. From the time of his taking his seat he became a constant attendant, and a club was formed of a considerable number of young men who had about the same time left the University and most of them entered into public life. The chief members were Mr. Pitt, Lord Euston, now Duke of Grafton, Lord Chatham, the Marquis of Graham, now Duke of Montrose, the Hon. Mr. Pratt, now Marquis of Camden, the Hon. St. Andrew St. John, Henry Bankes, Esq., the Hon. Maurice Robinson, now Lord Rokeby, Lord Duncannon, now Lord Bessborough, Lord Herbert, postea Earl of Pembroke, Lord Althorp, now Lord Spencer, Robert Smith, Esq., now Lord Carrington, Mr. Bridgeman, Mr. Steele, several others, and myself. To these were soon afterwards added Lord Apsley, Mr. Grenville, now Lord Grenville, Pepper Arden, afterwards Lord Alvanley, Charles Long, afterwards Lord Farnborough, Sir William Molesworth, &c. &c. Of the whole number Mr. Pitt was perhaps the most constant attendant, and as we frequently dined, and still more frequently supped together, and as our Parliamentary attendance gave us so many occasions for mutual conference and discussion, our acquaintance grew into great intimacy. Mr. Bankes and I (Lord Westmoreland only excepted, with whom, on account of his politics, Mr. Pitt had little connection) were the only members of the society who had houses of their own, Mr. Bankes in London, and I at Wimbolton[1] in Surrey. Mr. Bankes often received his friends to dinner at his own house, and they frequently visited me in the country, but more in the following Parliamentary session or two. In the spring of one of these years Mr. Pitt, who was remarkably fond of sleeping in the country, and would often go out of town for that purpose as late as eleven or twelve o'clock at night, slept at Wimbolton for two or three months together. It was, I believe, rather at a later period that he often used to sleep also at Mr. Robert Smith's house at Hamstead.[2]

Mr. Pitt was not long in the House of Commons before he took a part in the debates: I was present the first time he spoke, and I well recollect the effect produced on the whole House; his friends had expected much from him, but he surpassed all their expectations, and Mr. Hatsell, the chief clerk and a few of the older members who recollected his father, declared that Mr. Pitt gave indications of being his superior. I remember to this day the

[1] Wimbledon.   [2] Hampstead.

great pain I suffered from finding myself compelled by my judgment to vote against him on the *second* occasion of his coming forward, when the question was whether some Commissioners of public accounts should, or should not, be members of Parliament: indeed I never can forget the mixed emotions I experienced when my feelings had all the warmth and freshness of early youth, between my admiration of his powers, my sympathy with his rising reputation, and hopes of his anticipated greatness, while I nevertheless deemed it my duty in this instance to deny him my support.

Mr. Pitt was a decided and warm opponent of Lord North's administration; so indeed were most of our society, though I occasionally supported him. From the first, however, I concurred with Mr. Pitt in opposing the American War, and we rejoiced together in putting an end to it in about March, 1782, when Lord North's ministry terminated; and after a painful, and I think considerable, interval, during which it was said the King had even talked of going over to Hanover, and was supposed at last to yield to the counsels of the Earl of Mansfield, a new administration was formed consisting of the Rockingham and Shelburne parties, the Marquis of Rockingham being First Lord of the Treasury, and Lord Shelburne and Mr. Fox the two Secretaries of State. But though the parties had combined together against their common enemy, no sooner had he been removed than mutual jealousies immediately began to show themselves between the Rockingham and Shelburne parties. I well remember attending by invitation at Mr. Thomas Townshend's, since Lord Sydney, with Mr. Pitt and most of the young members who had voted with the Opposition, when Mr. Fox with apparent reluctance stated that Lord Rockingham had not then been admitted into the King's presence, but had only received communications through Lord Shelburne; and little circumstances soon afterwards arose which plainly indicated the mutual distrust of the two parties. Lord Rockingham's constitution was much shaken, and after a short illness his death took place before the end of the session of Parliament, about the middle of June, 1782.[1] Mr. Pitt had taken occasion to declare in the House of Commons that he would accept no subordinate situation, otherwise there is no doubt he would have been offered a seat at the Treasury Board, or indeed any office out of the Cabinet; but on Lord Rockingham's death, notwithstanding Mr. Fox's endeavour to prevent a rupture by declaring that *no disunion existed*,[2] the disagreement between the

---

[1] Here Mr. Wilberforce adds a pencilled note: "Devonshire House Ball. King."

[2] Mr. Wilberforce has written over this in pencil: "Qy.—Not a stroke of Providence could sever."

parties, of which so many symptoms had before manifested themselves, became complete and notorious. Lord Shelburne being invited by the King to supply Lord Rockingham's place, Mr. Fox with most of the Rockingham party retired from office, and Mr. Pitt accepted the offer made him by Lord Shelburne of becoming Chancellor of the Exchequer: he had completed his twenty-third year the 28th of May preceding.

There was more than one day of debate even during that session, in which Mr. Pitt indicated that gravity and dignity which became the high station which he had assumed at so early an age. He continued in office till the ensuing winter, when, after peace had been made both with America and her continental allies France and Spain, Lord Shelburne's administration was removed through the unprincipled coalition between Lord North and Mr. Fox and their respective parties. It was supposed to have been brought about in a great degree through the influence of Lord North's eldest son, who had maintained a friendly acquaintance with Mr. Fox, a man the fascination of whose manners and temper was such as to render it impossible for any one to maintain a personal intercourse with him without conceiving for him sincere and even affectionate attachment. I seconded the motion for the address on the peace, and I well remember a little before the business began writing a note in my place with a pencil to Bankes, who was, I saw, at a little distance, inquiring of him whether a union between North and Fox was really formed, and whether I might publicly notice it; "Yes," he replied, "the more strongly the better." Mr. Pitt on that night was very unwell; he was obliged to retire from the House into Solomon's Porch by a violent sickness at the very moment when Mr. Fox was speaking. He himself afterwards replied in a speech of some hours' length, but he certainly on that night fell short of our expectations; a second discussion, however, took place a few days after, and his speech on that occasion was one of the finest that was ever made in Parliament, both in point of argument and power of oratory. I never shall forget the impression produced by that part of it in which he spoke of his own retirement, closing with that passage out of Horace, "Laudo manentem," &c., though I must add that I retain no recollection whatever of the circumstance mentioned by Sir N. Wraxall; indeed I cannot but be strongly persuaded that he must have been misinformed. Well also do I remember our all going to Mr. Pitt's from the House of Commons after our defeat about eight in the morning, where a dinner had been waiting for us from eleven or twelve the preceding night, and where we all laughed heartily at some characteristic traits exhibited by Lord Stanhope,[1] then Lord Mahon. An administration was then formed of which the Duke of Portland was at the head, and Lord North and Mr. Fox joint Secretaries of State. It was in the autumn of this year, 1783, during the recess of Parliament, that I accompanied Mr. Pitt and Mr. Eliot, who afterwards became his brother-in-law, to France: our plan was to spend a few weeks in a provincial town, there to acquire something of the language, and afterwards to make a short stay at Paris. Accordingly we went to Rheims, where we continued for about six weeks. It was not until we were on the point of going abroad (when Mr. Eliot came out of Cornwall, Mr. Pitt from seeing his mother in Somersetshire, and I met them both at Sittingbourne) that we recollected that we were unprovided with letters of recommendation, which each of the party had perhaps trusted to the other for obtaining. Accordingly we requested Mr. Smith to obtain them for us of Mr. Thellusson, afterwards Lord Rendlesham, who, we knew, had correspondencies all over France. Thellusson replied that he would gladly do his best for us, but that he rather conceived from circumstances that his correspondent at Rheims was not a person of any

[1] Mr. Wilberforce has erased here " for desiring Mr. Pitt before he went out to pass his register bills."

commercial distinction. We, however, abided by our decision in favour of Rheims. The day after we arrived there, having sent our letter of recommendation the preceding evening to the person to whom it was addressed, we were waited upon by a very well-behaved man with a velvet coat, a bag, and sword, who conversed with us for a short time. The next day we repaid his visit, and were a good deal surprised to find that he was a very little grocer, his very small shop being separated by a partition from his very small room. But he was an unaffected, well-behaved man, and he offered to render us every service in his power, but stated distinctly that he was not acquainted with the higher people of the place and neighbourhood. For a few days we lived very comfortably together, but no French was learned except from the grammar, we not having a single French acquaintance. At length we desired our friend the *épicier* to mention us to the Lieutenant of Police, who, I think we had made out, had been employed to collect evidence in the great Douglas cause, and was therefore likely to know something of our country and its inhabitants. This expedient answered its intended purpose, though somewhat slowly and by degrees. The Lieutenant of Police, Du Chatel, an intelligent and apparently a respectable family man, came to visit us, and he having stated to the Archbishop of

Rheims, the present Cardinal de Perigord, whose palace was about a mile from the city, that three English Members of Parliament were then residing in it, one of whom was Mr. Pitt, who had recently been Chancellor of the Exchequer, his Grace sent his Grand Vicaire, the Abbé de la Garde, to ascertain the truth or falsehood of this statement. The Abbé executed his commission with great address, and reporting in our favour, we soon received an invitation to the Archbishop's table, followed by the expression of a wish that during the remainder of our stay at Rheims we would take up our residence in his palace. This we declined, but we occasionally dined with him, and from the time of our having been noticed by the Lieutenant we received continual invitations, chiefly to supper, from the gentry in and about the place. They were chiefly persons whose land produced the wine of the country, which, without scruple, they sold on their own account. And I remember the widow of the former Marshal Detrée intimating a wish that Mr. Pitt would become her customer.

Thence we went to Paris, having an opportunity during that time of spending four or five days at Fontainebleau, where the whole Court was assembled. There we were every evening at the parties of one or other of the French Ministers, in whose apartments we also dined—the Queen being always among the company present in the evening, and mixing in conversation with the greatest affability; there were also Madame la Princesse de Lamballe, M. Segur, M. de Castres, &c. Mr. George Ellis, who spoke French admirably, was in high favour for the elegance of his manners and the ease and brilliancy of his wit; and Mr. Pitt, though his imperfect knowledge of French prevented his doing justice to his sentiments, was yet able to give some impression of his superior powers—his language, so far as it did extend, being remarkable, I was assured, for its propriety and purity. There M. le Marquis de la Fayette appeared with a somewhat affected simplicity of manner, and I remember the fine ladies on one occasion dragging him to the card-table, while he shrugged up his shoulders and apparently resisted their importunities that he would join their party: very few, however, played at cards, the Queen, I think, never. During our stay at Paris we dined one day with M. le Marquis de la Fayette with a very small party, one of whom was Dr. Franklin; and it is due to M. le Marquis de la Fayette to declare that the opinion which we all formed of his principles and sentiments, so far as such a slight acquaintance could enable us to form a judgment, was certainly favourable, and his family appeared to be conducted more in the style of an English house than any other French family which we visited. We commonly supped in different parties, and I recollect one night when we English manifested our too common indisposition to conform ourselves to foreign customs, or rather to put ourselves out of our own way, by all going together to one table, to the number of twelve or fourteen of us, and admitting only one Frenchman, the Marquis de Noailles, M. de la Fayette's brother-in-law, who spoke our own language like an Englishman, and appeared more than any of the other French to be one of ourselves. We, however, who were all young men, were more excusable than our Ambassador at the Court of France, who, I remember, joined our party.

It was at Paris, in October, that Mr. Pitt first became acquainted with Mr. Rose, who was introduced to him by Lord Thurlow, whose fellow-traveller he was on the Continent; and it was then, or immediately afterwards, that it was suggested to the late Lord Camden by Mr. Walpole, a particular friend of M. Necker's, that if Mr. Pitt should be disposed to offer his hand to Mademoiselle N., afterwards Madame de Staël, such was the respect entertained for him by M. and Madame Necker, that he had no doubt the proposal would be accepted.

We returned from France about November. Circumstances then soon commenced which issued in the turning out of the Fox administration, the King resenting grievously, as was said, the treatment he experienced from them, especially in what regarded the settlement of the Prince of Wales. I need only allude to the long course of political contention which took place in the winter of 1783-84, when at length Mr. Pitt became First Lord of the Treasury; and after a violent struggle, the King dissolved the Parliament about March, and in the new House of Commons a decisive majority attested the truth of Mr. Pitt's assertion that he possessed the confidence of his country. In many counties and cities the friends of Mr. Fox were turned out, thence denominated Fox's Martyrs.[1] I myself became member for Yorkshire in the place of Mr. Foljambe, Sir George Savile's nephew, who had succeeded that excellent public man in the representation of the county not many weeks before. I may be allowed to take this occasion of mentioning a circumstance honourable to myself, since it is much more honourable to him, that some years after he came to York on purpose to support me in my contest for the county. It is remarkable that Lord Stanhope first foresaw the necessity there would be for Mr. Pitt's continuing in office notwithstanding his being out-voted in the

[1] Mr. Wilberforce has written here in pencil on the margin, "Fox's Martyrs. Qy. number."

House of Commons, maintaining that the Opposition would not venture to refuse the supplies, and that at the proper moment he should dissolve the Parliament.[1]

And now having traced Mr. Pitt's course from childhood to the period when he commenced his administration of sixteen or seventeen years during times the most stormy and dangerous almost ever experienced by this country, it may be no improper occasion for describing his character, and specifying the leading talents, dispositions, and qualifications by which he was distinguished. But before I proceed to this delineation it may be right to mention that seldom has any man had a better opportunity of knowing another than I have possessed of being thoroughly acquainted with Mr. Pitt. For weeks and months together I have spent hours with him every morning while he was transacting his common business with his secretaries. Hundreds of times, probably, I have called him out of bed, and have, in short, seen him in every situation and in his most unreserved moments. As he knew I should not ask anything of him, and as he reposed so much confidence in me as to be persuaded that I should

[1] Mr. Wilberforce adds here a pencil note in his own handwriting: "Remarkable that when I entered York, in order to attend a public meeting which was about to take place, there was but one gentleman with whom I had the smallest acquaintance, the Rev. Wm. Mason, the poet."

never use any information I might obtain from him for any unfair purpose, he talked freely before me of men and things, of actual, meditated, or questionable appointments and plans, projects, speculations, &c., &c. No man, it has been said, is a hero to his *valet de chambre*, and if, with all the opportunities I enjoyed of seeing Mr. Pitt in his most inartificial and unguarded moments, he nevertheless appeared to me to be a man of extraordinary intellectual and moral powers, it is due to him that it should be known that this opinion was formed by one in whose instance Mr. Pitt's character was subjected to its most severe test, which Rochefoucault appeared to think could be stood by no human hero.

Mr. Pitt's intellectual powers were of the highest order, and in private no less than in public, when he was explaining his sentiments in any complicated question and stating the arguments on both sides, it was impossible not to admire the clearness of his conceptions, the precision with which he contemplated every particular object, and a variety of objects, without confusion. They who have had occasion to discuss political questions with him in private will acknowledge that there never was a fairer reasoner, never any one more promptly recognising, and allowing its full weight to every consideration and argument which was urged against the opinion he had embraced. You always saw *where* you differed from him and *why*. The difference arose commonly from his sanguine temper leading him to give credit to information which others might distrust, and to expect that doubtful contingencies would have a more favourable issue than others might venture to anticipate. I never met with any man who combined in an equal degree this extraordinary precision of understanding with the same intuitive apprehension of every shade of opinion, or of feeling, which might be indicated by those with whom he was conversant. In taking an estimate of Mr. Pitt's intellectual powers, his extraordinary memory ought to be specially noticed. It was indeed remarkable for two excellencies which are seldom found united in the same person—a facility of receiving impressions, and a firmness and precision in retaining them. His great rival, Mr. Fox, was also endowed with a memory which to myself used to appear perfectly wonderful. Often in the earlier part of my Parliamentary life I have heard him (Fox) at a very late hour speak, without having taken any notes, for two or three hours, noticing every material argument that had been urged by every speaker of the opposite party : this he commonly did in the order in which those arguments had been delivered, whereas it was rather Mr. Pitt's habit to form the plan of a speech in his mind while the debate was going forward, and to distribute his comments on the various statements and remarks of his opponents according to the arrangement which he had made. Such was his (Pitt's) recollection of the great classical authors of antiquity that scarcely a passage could be quoted of their works, whether in verse or prose, with which he was not so familiar as to be able to take up the clue and go on with what immediately followed. This was particularly the case in the works of Virgil, Horace, and Cicero, and I am assured that he was also scarcely less familiar with Homer and Thucydides.

He had considerable powers of imagination and much ready wit, but this quality appeared more to arise from every idea, and every expression that belonged to it, being at once present to his mind, so as to enable him at will to make such combinations as suited the purpose of the moment, than as if his mind was only conscious at the time of that particular coruscation which the collision of objects caused to flash before the mental eye. It arose out of this distinctive peculiarity that he was not carried away by his own wit, though he could at any time command its exercise, and no man, perhaps, at proper seasons ever indulged more freely or happily in that playful facetiousness which gratifies all without wounding any. He had great natural courage and fortitude, and though always of a disordered stomach and gouty tendencies (on account of which port wine had been recommended to him in his earliest youth, and drinking French wine for a day or two would at any time produce gouty pains in the extremities), yet his bodily temperament never produced the smallest appearance of mental weakness or sinking. I think it was from this source, combined with that of his naturally sanguine temper, that though manifestly showing how deeply he felt on public affairs, he never was harassed or distressed by them, and till his last illness, when his bodily powers were almost utterly exhausted, his inward emotions never appeared to cloud his spirits, or affect his temper. Always he was ready in the little intervals of a busy man to indulge in those sallies of wit and good humour which were naturally called forth.

Excepting only the cases of those who have had reason to apprehend the loss of life or liberty, never was a public man in circumstances more harassing than those of Mr. Pitt in 1784: for several weeks the fate of his administration and that of his opponents were trembling on the beam, sometimes one scale preponderating, sometimes the other; almost daily it appeared doubtful whether he was to continue Prime Minister or retire into private life. Yet though then not five-and-twenty I do not believe that the anxiety of his situation ever kept him awake for a single minute, or ever appeared to sadden or cast a gloom over his hours of relaxation

It cannot perhaps be affirmed that he was altogether free from pride, but great natural shyness,[1] and even awkwardness (French *gaucherie*), often produced effects for which pride was falsely charged on him; and really that confidence which might be justly placed in his own powers by a man who could not but be conscious of their superiority might sometimes appear like pride, though not fairly deserving that appellation; and this should be the rather conceded, because from most of the acknowledged effects of pride upon the character he was eminently free. No man, as I have already remarked, ever listened more attentively to what was stated against his own opinions; no man appeared to feel more for others when in distress; no man was ever more kind and indulgent to his inferiors and dependents of every class, and never were there any of those little acts of superciliousness, or indifference to the feelings and comforts of others, by which secret pride is sometimes betrayed. But if Mr. Pitt was not wholly free from pride, it may truly be affirmed that no man was perhaps ever more devoid of vanity in all its forms. One particular more in Mr. Pitt's character, scarcely ever found in a proud man, was the extraordinary good humour and candour with which he explained and discussed any plan or

[1] Here there is a pencil note: "For he was one of the shyest men I ever knew."

measure, of which he had formed the outline in his mind, with those professional men who were necessarily to be employed in giving it a Parliamentary form and language. I do not believe that there is a single professional man or the head of any board who ever did business with him, who would not acknowledge that he was on such occasions the most easy and accommodable man with whom they ever carried on official intercourse. One instance of this kind shall be mentioned as a specimen of the others. He had formed a plan of importance (I think in some Revenue matter) on which it was necessary for him to consult with the Attorney-General of the day, I believe Chief Baron Macdonald; Mr. Pitt had been for some time ruminating on the measure, his mind had been occupied for perhaps a month in moulding it into form and in devising expedients for its more complete execution. It may here be not out of place to mention as a peculiarity of his character that he was habitually apt to have almost his whole thoughts and attention and time occupied with the particular object or plan which he was then devising and wishing to introduce into practice. He was as usual full of his scheme, and detailed it to his professional friend with the warmth and ability natural to him on such occasions. But the Attorney-General soon became convinced that there were legal objections to the measure, which must be decisive against its adoption. These therefore he explained to Mr. Pitt, who immediately gave up his plan with the most unruffled good-humour, without attempting to hang by it, or to devise methods of propping it up, but, casting it at once aside, he pursued his other business as cheerfully and pleasantly as usual.

But there are many who with undisturbed composure and with a good grace can on *important* occasions thus change their line of conduct and assume a course contrary to that which they would have preferred. It is, however, far more rare to find men who on little occasions, which are not of sufficient moment to call a man's dignity into action, and which are not under the public eye, can bear to have their opinions opposed and their plans set aside, without manifesting some irritation or momentary fretfulness. But on the lesser scale as well as on the greater Mr. Pitt's good-humour was preserved. This same disposition of mind was attended with the most important advantages, and in truth was one which eminently qualified him to be the Minister of a free country.

If towards the latter end of his life his temper was not so entirely free from those occasional approaches to fretfulness which continued disease and the necessity of struggling against it too often produce, it ought to be taken into account that another powerful cause besides human infirmity might have tended to lessen that kindness and good-humour for which he was for the greater part of his life so remarkable. The deference that was paid to him was justly great, but though no man less than himself exacted anything like servility from his companions, it is impossible to deny that there were those who attempted to cultivate his favour by this species of adulation. Another particular in Mr. Pitt, seldom connected with pride, was the kind interest he took in the rising talents of every young public man of any promise whose politics were congenial with his own; as well as the justice which he did to the powers of his opponents—a quality which it is but fair to say was no less apparent in Mr. Fox also. If he sometimes appeared to be desirous of letting a debate come to a close without hearing some friends who wished to take a part in it, this arose in some degree in his wishing to get away, from his being tired out with Parliamentary speaking and hearing, or from thinking that the debate would close more advantageously at the point at which he stopped.

In society he was remarkably cheerful and pleasant, full of wit and playfulness, neither, like Mr. Fox, fond of arguing a question, nor yet holding forth, like some others.[1] He was always ready to hear others as well as to talk himself.

[1] Pencil note: "Wyndham."

In very early life he now and then engaged in games of chance, and the vehemence with which he was animated was certainly very great; but finding that he was too much interested by them, all at once he entirely and for life desisted from gambling.

His regard for truth was greater than I ever saw in any man who was not strongly under the influence of a powerful principle of religion: he appeared to adhere to it out of respect to himself, from a certain moral purity which appeared to be a part of his nature. A little incident may afford an example of his delicacy in this respect. A common friend of ours, a member of the House of Lords, was reflected upon with considerable acrimony in the House of Commons by one of Mr. Pitt's political opponents. Being with him, as often happened, the next morning, while he was at breakfast, I told him that the animadversions which had been made on our friend the night before were stated in the newspaper, and I expressed some surprise that he himself had not contradicted the fact which was the ground of the reprehension. "This," said he, "I might have done, but you will remember that it was a circumstance in which, if I deviated from strict truth, no other man could know of it, and in such a case it is peculiarly requisite to keep within the strictest limits of veracity."

The remark I am about to make may deserve the more attention on account of its general application, and because it may probably tend to illustrate other characters. It may, I believe, be truly affirmed that the imputations which were sometimes thrown out against Mr. Pitt, that he was wanting in simplicity and frankness, and the answers he made to questions put to him concerning his future conduct, or the principles which were regulating the course of measures he pursued, were in truth a direct consequence of that very strictness and veracity for which he was so remarkable. When men are not very scrupulous as to truth, they naturally deal in broad assertions, especially in cases in which their feelings are at all warmly engaged; but it seldom happens that a political man can thus assume a principle and apply it to all the cases, which, in the use he is about to make of it, it may be supposed to comprehend, without some qualifications and distinctions; and a man of strict veracity therefore makes a conditional declaration or gives a qualified assurance. The same remark applies to the judgments we may express of the character and conduct of public men. In order to be strictly correct we cannot always use broad and strong colouring, but there must be shades and gradations in our draught. Yet such is the natural and even commendable love which men generally have of truth and honesty, that we feel an instinctive preference of simple and strong affirmations or negations as indicating more blunt and straightforward principles and dispositions, than where men express themselves in measured and qualified and conditional propositions. No man, I believe, ever loved his country with a warmer or more sincere affection; it was highly gratifying to converse familiarly with him on the plans he was forming for the public good; or to witness the pleasure he experienced from indulging speculations of the benefits which his country might derive from the realising of such or such a hope.

But notwithstanding all my admiration of Mr. Pitt's extraordinary powers, and still more, with the deepest and most assured conviction of his public spirit and patriotism, I cannot but think that even his uncommon excellencies were not without some alloy of human infirmity. In particular he appeared to me to be defective in his knowledge of human nature, or that from some cause or other he was less sagacious than might have been expected from his superior talents, in his estimate of future events, and sometimes in his judgment of character. This might probably arise in part from his naturally sanguine temper, which in estimating future contingencies might lead him to assign too little weight to those probabilities which were opposed to his ultimate conclusion. But if I must be honest in delineating Mr. Pitt's character and qualities, I must also confess that in considering their practical influence on the fortunes of his country, I have sometimes been almost ready to believe that powers far inferior to his, under the direction of a mind equally sincere and equally warm in its zeal for the public good, might have been the instrument of conferring far greater benefits on his country. His great qualities, under the impulse and guidance of true religion, would probably have been the means of obtaining for his country much greater temporal blessings, together with others of a far higher order, and more durable effects. The circumstances of the period at which he first came into the situation of Prime Minister were such as almost to invest him with absolute power. All his faculties then possessed the bloom of youthful beauty as well as the full vigour of maturer age: his mind was ardent, his principles were pure, his patriotism warm, his mind as yet altogether unsullied by habitually associating with men of worldly ways of thinking and acting, in short, with a class which may be not unfitly termed trading politicians; this is a class with which perhaps no one, however originally pure, can habitually associate, especially in the hours of friendly intercourse and of social recreation, without contracting insensibly more or less defilement. No one who had not been an eye-witness could conceive the ascendency which Mr. Pitt then possessed over the House of Commons, and if he had then generously adopted the resolution to govern his country by *principle* rather than by *influence*, it was a resolution which he could then have carried into execution with success, and the full effects of which, both on the national character, interests, and happiness, it is scarcely possible perhaps to estimate; but it would be a curious and no unprofitable speculation to trace the probable effects which would have resulted from the assumption of this high moral tone, in the actual circumstances of this country, in reference both to our internal interests and our foreign relations. This is a task I cannot now undertake, but I may remind the reader that the principles were then beginning to propagate themselves with the greatest success which not long after exhibited their true nature and ruinous effects in the French Revolution. Such a spirit of patriotism would have been kindled, such a generous confidence in the King's government would have been diffused throughout all classes, that the very idea of the danger of our being infected with the principles of French licentiousness, which might have produced among our people a general taint of disloyalty, would have been an apprehension not to be admitted into the bosom of the most timid politician; while the various reforms which would have taken place, and the manifest independence of Parliament would have generated and ensured in the minds of all reasonable men a continually increasing gratitude and affection for the constitution and laws of our country. On the other hand, the French, infatuated as they were, and wicked as were the men who then possessed the chief influence in the counsels of that country, could never have been so blind to their own manifest interest, as to have engaged their people in a war with Great Britain from any idea of our confederating with the Crowned Heads of Europe to crush the rising spirit of liberty in France. Hence we should have escaped that long and bloody war, which, however, in its ultimate issue justly deserving the epithet of glorious, is nevertheless the cause of all our present dangers and sufferings, from the insupportable burdens with which it has loaded us. Nor is it only *Financial* evils of which our long protracted warfare has been the cause; to this source also we must probably trace much of that *Moral* evil, which in so many different forms has been of late beginning to manifest itself, especially among the lower orders of our people. The gracious Providence of God has indeed abundantly answered the prayers of many among us, who I trust have all along been looking up to the Giver of all Good for their country's safety and prosperity; and while those causes were in operation which were hereafter to manifest themselves in various forms of social and domestic evil, it pleased God to diffuse a spirit of an opposite kind, which began to display its love of God and love of man by the formation of societies of a religious and moral nature, which have already contributed in no small degree to bless almost all nations, while they have invested our own country with a moral glory never before enjoyed by any nation upon earth. The diffusion of the Sacred Scriptures, the establishment of societies for spreading throughout the world the blessings of religious light and of moral improvement, the growing attention to the education of our people, with societies and institutions for relieving every species of suffering which vice and misery can ever produce among the human race,—what would have been the effects of all this, if not obstructed and counteracted in all the various ways by which war, that greatest scourge of the human race, carries on its baleful and wide wasting operations.[1]

Is it not a melancholy consideration that this very country, the constitution and laws of which have been the objects of the highest possible

[1] A note: "Vary here."

admiration of the wisest men, should be in such a state that but too large a part of the great body of our people, instead of looking up to Heaven with gratitude for being favoured with blessings never before enjoyed by any nation, should be led by their sufferings to regard that very constitution and those very laws with disgust and aversion? Of this unhappy state of things the war, as having been the cause of our financial distresses and difficulties, is in fact the source. But there is nothing in which we are so apt to deceive ourselves as in conceiving that we are capable of estimating the full amount of moral good or evil; short-sighted as we are, there is nothing in which our views are more manifestly narrow and contracted; an important, nay, an awful consideration, which, while it may well encourage to activity in all good, should make us tremble to admit (the slightest speck) the smallest seed of moral evil to pollute our country's soil. But I have been led to expatiate more than I intended on this topic, though merely glancing at some of the most important of the considerations which it presents to the view even of the most superficial observer.

Returning to the consideration of the effect of true religion on the character and conduct of the great man who has been the subject of this inquiry, I am naturally led to remark that there can be no possible occasion on which the application of the principle on which I have been lately speaking would suggest wider scope for our reflection. But if we consider the effect which true religion would have produced either in himself or in others around him, how immense would appear the mass of benefits, in the employment of his time, in the application of his faculties, in the selection of his companions, perhaps, above all, in his giving their just weight to religious and moral principles and character in the exercise of his unlimited patronage, both in Church and State ; and considering that every religious and good man, who by him should have been invested with power and influence, would *himself* have selected others of similar principles and character, throughout the descending series of official appointments, and through all the variety of social occupations, who can say what would have been the effect of these religious and moral secretions, if they may be so termed, which throughout the whole political body would have been gradually producing their blessed effects in augmenting its fulness, symmetry, and strength?[1] And these effects, remember, would have been of a merely public, still less of a merely political character. They would have been, to say the least, full *as* manifest, and even more fertile in the production

[1] A note :—" Dilate, and Figure."

of happiness in all the walks of private life and all the varieties of social combination.

In considering the estimates which were formed of Mr. Pitt's and Mr. Fox's characters respectively, more especially in point of what may be called popularity; and also as to their reputation for genius, wit, and classical taste, it should be remembered that Mr. Fox happened to have become connected, both at school and at Oxford, with a circle of men eminent for talents and classical proficiency, men also who were not shut up in cloisters, but who lived in the world, and gave the tone in the highest and most polished societies of the metropolis. Among these were Mr. Hare, General Fitzpatrick, Lord John Townshend; and to these must be added Mr. Windham, Mr. Erskine, and, above all, Mr. Sheridan. Mr. Pitt had also several college friends who came into Parliament about the same period with himself, men of no inferior consideration—Mr. Bankes, Mr. Eliot, Lord Abercorn, Lord Spencer, and several others. But these, it must be confessed, were by no means men of the same degree of brilliancy as the former set; nor did they in the same degree live in the circle of fashion and there diffuse their own opinions. Again Mr. Fox's political connections were numerous, and such as naturally tended to stamp a high value on his character. Burke, Barré—for there were those

THE RIGHT HONBLE. WILLIAM PITT.

also who though not of Fox's party, often associated with him in private, and tended to sustain the general estimate of his superiority; of these were Gibbon, Lord Thurlow, Dunning, Jeykell.

Again, the necessity under which Mr. Pitt often lay of opening and speaking upon subjects of a low and vulgarising quality, such as the excise on tobacco, wine, &c., &c., topics almost incapable with propriety, of an association with wit or grace, especially in one who was so utterly devoid of all disposition to seek occasions for shining, tended to produce a real mediocrity of sentiment and a lack of ornament, as well as to increase the impression that such was the nature of his oratory. Also the speeches of a minister were of necessity more guarded, and his subjects, except where he was opening some new proposition or plan, were rather prescribed to him by others, than selected by himself.[1]

. . . .

The MS. of Canning's lines on Pitt is amongst the Wilberforce Papers; they are so little known that no apology is needed for inserting them here. Canning wrote them for the feast in honour of Pitt's birthday, May 28, 1802. It will be remembered that Pitt had resigned in 1801, because the King would not accept his Irish policy. A vote of cen-

[1] Here is added in pencil, "2nd Nov. 1821."

sure had been moved, and was not merely rejected, but, by an overwhelming majority, it was carried " that the Right Hon. William Pitt has rendered great and important services to his country, and especially deserved the gratitude of this House."[1]

THE PILOT THAT WEATHER'D THE STORM.

(A Song written in 1802.)

If hush'd the loud whirlwind that ruffled the deep,
    The sky, if no longer dark tempests deform;
When our perils are past, shall our gratitude sleep?
    No! Here's to the Pilot that weather'd the storm!

At the footstool of Power let flattery fawn,
    Let faction her idols extol to the skies;
To Virtue, in humble retirement withdrawn,
    Unblam'd may the merits of gratitude rise.

And shall not his memory to Britain be dear,
    Whose example with envy all nations behold;
A Statesman unbias'd by int'rest or fear,
    By pow'r uncorrupted, untainted by gold?

Who, when terror and doubt through the universe reigned,
    While rapine and treason their standards unfurl'd,
The heart and the hopes of his country maintained,
    And one kingdom preserv'd midst the wreck of the world.

Unheeding, unthankful, we bask in the blaze,
    While the beams of the sun in full majesty shine;
When he sinks into twilight, with fondness we gaze,
    And mark the mild lustre that gilds his decline.

[1] Rosebery's " Life of Pitt," p. 233.

SKETCH OF PITT

Lo! Pitt, when the course of thy greatness is o'er,
   Thy talents, thy virtues, we fondly recall!
Now justly we prize thee, when lost we deplore;
   Admir'd in thy zenith, but lov'd in thy fall.

Oh! take, then—for dangers by wisdom repelled,
   For evils, by courage and constancy brav'd—
Oh take! for a throne by thy counsels upheld
   The thanks of a people thy firmness has sav'd.

And oh! if again the rude whirlwind should rise!
   The dawning of peace should fresh darkness deform,
The regrets of the good, and the fears of the wise,
   Shall turn to the Pilot that weather'd the storm

LETTERS FROM FRIENDS

The letters which follow are from friends of Wilberforce between the years 1786-1832: they touch on a variety of subjects. George Rose[1] writes in 1790 in the full flush of excitement on the news of "peace certain and unequivocal on the very terms prescribed from hence."

---

[1] Then Clerk of Parliaments. Rose writes to Wilberforce later: "I shall never find words, either in speaking or writing, to express what I think of you."

LETTERS FROM FRIENDS

Right Hon. George Rose to Mr. Wilberforce.
"OLD PALACE YARD,
"*November* 4, 1790.

"MY DEAR WILBERFORCE,—I was shocked this morning in putting my papers in order on my table to find a letter I wrote to you before I went into the country; you must have thought me shamefully inattentive to you, which I trust I never shall be while I retain my senses, for anxious as I am to avoid such an imputation in general I do assure you I am particularly so to stand clear of that in your opinion. I will now, however, make you ample amends for the seeming neglect by telling you that the expected messenger is arrived and brings us an account of peace *certain* and *unequivocal*, on the very terms (I may say to you) *prescribed* from hence; they secure to us great and essential points important to the interests of the country, and must prevent future occasions of quarrel with Spain; war with all its certain and possible consequences are (*sic*) avoided. So much for public benefits; what it must produce to the individual[1] to whom the merit is justly and fairly to be ascribed it is impossible at once to foresee—I mean with respect to character of everything that can be valuable to a man in his situation.

"I have actually been drunk ever since ten o'clock this morning, and have not yet quite the use of my reason, but I am

"Yours most faithfully and cordially,

"GEORGE ROSE."

Pitt's views as to a bounty on corn in the scarcity then[2] prevailing are given by Rose in the next letter.

Right Hon. G. Rose to Mr. Wilberforce.

"MY DEAR WILBERFORCE,—It would be very odd if your writing to me on the subject of your last, or indeed on any other, could require an apology; I regret only that I cannot give you the light upon it you wish.

"With respect to measures within the reach of Government to relieve the scarcity I fear none can be effectual. Mr. Pitt cannot, as you know, after his declaration in Parliament, import at the

---

[1] Pitt. [2] About 1802.

expense or risk of the public, but he is inclined to give a bounty on corn imported when it shall be *below* a certain price within a limited time. This is a new principle, but I really believe it would produce much good. The idea occurred to him on reading Mr. Richardson's letter to you, who stated the great discouragement of individuals importing to be the risk of prices being low on the arrival of cargoes in the spring; I was so much struck with Mr. Richardson's observations that I wrote to beg him to call on me last Monday, but he had unfortunately set off that morning for Liverpool. I am more than half disposed to take the chance of prevailing with him to come up again.

"During our late sitting the Scotch distilleries were stopped, but the prices of barley in England were not *then* such as to induce any man to hint even at the English; and of course there is now no power to prevent them going on. We did prohibit the distillation of wheat; and allowed the importation of starch at the Home Duty, which will stop that manufactory; but I deplore most sincerely and earnestly any agreement against the use of hair powder, not merely for the sake of a large revenue, but to avoid other mischief which I am very sure is not enough attended to, the distinction of dress and external appearance.

The inattention to that has been a great support of Jacobinism.

"The resolutions which were taken in the last scarcity for restraining the use of flour, &c., were so little attended, and were on the whole productive of so little good that Mr. Pitt has not thought it yet advisable to recur to them. I believe *much* may be done, especially in towns, by soup shops, respecting which I should think Mr. Bernard can inform you as fully as any one, from the share he took in the conduct of them in London last winter. Perhaps the article may be made somewhat cheaper here than anywhere else from there being a larger quantity of coarse parts of the meat than in any country place, but the soup was made admirably good, palatable and nutritive for twopence a quart, and retailed at half that price; one pint an ample allowance for each person, taking adults and children together, so that for one halfpenny a day a comfortable mess was provided for a poor person. I am making the experiment both at Christ Church and Lyndhurst and I shall soon see how it will answer. I am not sure but that some general plan of that sort will be as likely as any other to be useful now. I think also of importing a cargo of corn now, as I did pork on the last occasion, and it may be a good thing to encourage others to do the same for the supply of their respective neighbourhoods, which people will be more disposed to do if Mr. Pitt should propose the bounty I have alluded to.

"The dry weather during the last twelve days I hope will be productive of infinite good; nothing could be more fortunate, as the seed I hope will now be all well got in, which may have an immediate effect in lowering the prices."

A letter of a later date from Rose follows as to the payment of Pitt's debts by subscription amongst his friends. Wilberforce was sanguine as to the success of this plan "considering the number of affluent men connected with Pitt, some of whom have got great and lucrative places from him." Wilberforce drew up a list of sixty-three persons who "might be expected to contribute." But the plan of a private subscription fell to the ground.

Right Hon. G. Rose to Mr. Wilberforce.

"OLD PALACE YARD,
"*January* 25, 1806, *Saturday*.

"MY DEAR WILBERFORCE,—I told you, immediately after the receipt of your former letters, that all thought of applying to Parliament for payment of Mr. Pitt's debts was abandoned; and measures are taking for the attainment of that object, which will be very greatly assisted by your endeavours I am sure. Mr. Samuel Thornton and Mr. Angerstein are to meet several gentlemen in the city on Tuesday morning to promote a private subscription, and whatever may be necessary to be done at this end of the town I trust will be effected. I hope I expressed myself intelligibly respecting your motives—you cannot be more certain of them than I am—and I felt deeply obliged by the plainness with which you expressed your sentiments; they decided my conduct instantly, as I told you before.

"As to the wish expressed by our late inestimable friend relative to the Stanhopes, I suggested to you that as provision had been made for the husbands of the two elder ones, equal to £1,000 a year, I believe, for each, I thought a further one by Parliament could hardly be acquiesced in. For Lady Hester I hoped no difficulty would be made in providing an annuity to that amount. The two young men are in the army—*they* are not of Mr. Pitt's blood—and small sinecure employments are given to them which will aid their income.

"Three gentlemen are to meet in the city on Monday to concert the best measures for promoting the subscription, and you shall know the result. You will, I am persuaded, come in to attend the House on that day.

"The Bishop of Lincoln is at the Deanery.

"I am, my dear Wilberforce,

"Most truly yours,

"George Rose."

The next two letters are from Dundas, afterwards Lord Melville,[1] "the only minister to whose judgment Pitt greatly deferred." Wilberforce writes of him as "an excellent man of business and a fine, warm-hearted fellow," but later on he says, "his connection with Dundas was Pitt's great misfortune."[2] The first letter is on the subject of free exports of our manufactures to Holland.

Right Hon. Henry Dundas to Mr. Wilberforce.

"WIMBLEDON, *August* 15, 1796.

"MY DEAR W.,—I have spoke both with Mr. Pitt and Lord Grenville on the subject of a free exportation of our manufactures from this country to Holland. I think they agree with me in thinking that if the restraint was ever a politick one the time is passed. Lord Liverpool, I believe, is of a different opinion, but it will immediately come under discussion, and I would hope he will act wisely upon it. For my own part, I am of opinion that it is a degree of infatuation at the present moment to prevent the trade and manufactures of the country finding an exit and a vent in any mode and by any channel the enterprise of the merchants can devise. I am as well as can be under all the anxieties which the state of the

[1] Lecky, vol. vii. p. 32.
[2] Dundas, who had been Treasurer to the Navy, was impeached on April 29, 1805, on a charge of misappropriating £10,000 worth of public money. He was acquitted June 12, 1805.

country naturally suggests, and the pain arising from that anxiety is not diminished by feeling oneself free from the blame of all the mischief which is going on. Who would have thought not many years ago that in the year 1796 Great Britain should be the only nation to be found true to its own interests, or in a situation to maintain them. But I find my pen running away with me, and must conclude with congratulating you on the fine weather and luxuriant crops, and with being, my dear Wil,

"Yours sincerely,

"HENRY DUNDAS."

Dundas's remarks on the defence of the country and the raising of volunteer and yeomanry corps in 1798 are not without interest in 1897.

"WIMBLEDON, *January* 29, 1798.

"MY DEAR WILBERFORCE,—There can not be a doubt of the wishes of Government to bring forward the zeal and exertions of the country in every practicable shape; at present I am not aware that any thing cheaper (if really efficient) can be resorted to than the system of volunteer corps and yeomanry corps to which every encouragement is given. At the same time if any proposal through the regular channel can be laid before Government having the same tendency, there can not be a doubt of its being duly attended to.

The only satisfactory answer therefore which I can make to your letter is to suggest to you the propriety of mentioning to your friends who have applied to you, that it would be best for them to put in writing the specified plan they would severally wish to adopt, and if that is sent to the Duke of Portland by the Lord Lieutenant, I have no reason to doubt that it will be duly attended to. If a copy of the proposal is at the same time extra officially laid before me, it might be the means of expediting the consideration of it, as I have frequent opportunities of conversing with the Dukes of York and Portland, and likewise with Mr. Pitt on all subjects of that nature. Indeed the proper defence of the country by every possible means it can be done with effect and economy occupies my unremitting attention, and if I observe it neglected in any department, it vexes and distresses me more than I can describe, and perhaps more than is convenient consistently with keeping one's mind in a constant tenor of steady and unruffled attention. I was sorry to learn within these two days that Mrs. Wilberforce is ailing, and

"I remain, my dear Wilberforce,
"Yours very sincerely,
"HENRY DUNDAS."

In his later days when he had withdrawn to

a great extent from the society which he had charmed in his youth Wilberforce's chief female friends were Hannah More, of whose letters hundreds remain, Martha More, Mrs. Fry, Maria Edgeworth. In strong contrast stand out the friendships of the youthful days, when Wilberforce's Wimbledon villa was the resort of witty and fashionable, rather than of learned and charitable ladies, when he was "sitting up all night singing" and when the society he frequented included Mrs. Siddons, Mrs. Crewe, Mrs. Sheridan, the Duchess of Portland, and last but not least, the beautiful and bewitching Jane Duchess of Gordon, she who raised the regiment of Gordon Highlanders by giving, as was said, the shilling from her mouth to the recruits.

The Duchess of Gordon writes to William Wilberforce in July, 1788, of "the many happy hours I have spent at Wimbledon," and from Keswick this versatile woman tells him of the "sweet church" she had passed by and how she "found myself repeating the lines, 'Remote from man with God he passed his days, Prayer all his business, all his pleasure praise': it is thus I should like to live, the world forgetting by the world forgot." She tries to tempt him to Gordon Castle in these words: "I know that 'silent glens have charms for thee,' and this is the country in which you will find those silent and peaceful abodes. Nature bestowed every wild, uncultivated beauty, with a purer air and brighter horizon. Here Hygeia is to be found; we lead the lives of hermits. Dr. Beattie shall be our companion. We go to bed at eleven, and sometimes visit the majestic ocean before breakfast. I am certain the air of this country would perfectly re-establish your health, which would give joy to thousands, and no one more than, &c.,

"J. GORDON."

In this letter the Duchess encloses her correspondence with Dundas, who was one of the circle at that Liberty Hall of Wimbledon.

The Duchess had had a misunderstanding with Dundas which she wished Wilberforce to heal through his influence with Pitt. She had "dropped some words" respecting Dundas to Pitt which had "got round" to the former. Dundas writes to her:

"INDIA OFFICE,
"*July* 4, 1788.

"DEAR DUCHESS,—I received your affectionate note previous to your departure for Scotland. A great part of its contents are more fit for discussion in free conversation than by letter. I have only to beg of you always to keep in remembrance the long letter I wrote to you in consequence of some words you dropped to Mr. Pitt respecting me last winter.

"It is scarcely possible for you to put me out of humour, because however much you may at times forget yourself, and get into sallies of unguarded expression, you would be almost the worst of beings if you was seriously to entertain for me any other sentiments than those of perfect regard and affection. I therefore never suspect you of any serious alteration of your regard. But let me for your own sake entreat you to reflect that everybody does not make the same allowance that I do. You judge truly when you think that you have many enemies, and be assured that there is no such good receipt for having enemies than to talk rashly or disrespectfully behind their backs; and be sure of it these things in some way or other get round, and no after-civility is received as an expiation. On the contrary, it brings upon you the imputation of duplicity which of all other ingredients in a character ought (even the suspicion of it) to be avoided.

"After so long a lecture, I think it right to console you with enclosing Sir George Young's note just received. I leave you to say anything you please about me to Mrs. Gordon, only let her not imagine that I made professions even in the middle of a country dance without a perfect determination to realise them. Remember me affectionately to everybody, and

"I remain,

"Yours sincerely,

"HENRY DUNDAS."

The Duchess's answer to Dundas is so full of piquancy that it helps one to realise the personality of this remarkable woman.

Duchess of Gordon to Right Hon. Henry Dundas.

"GORDON CASTLE,

"*July* 13, 1788.

"I have this morning yours, and though not a little confused with the bustle of joy that surrounds me, cannot delay answering it. There is something in the strain of your letters so unlike the ideas that you convey in our conversation that I cannot think they are wrote by the same person.

"Why mention duplicity to me? You know there is not a human being further from it; and I know you don't in your heart believe one word upon the subject. If you do, you have not the penetration the world gives you; for I can assure you with the firmest confidence you are most egregiously mistaken. It would be better for me if I had a little more of that detestable vice, or even the policy to conceal my sentiments, for I am convinced my enemies are the offspring of too much openness; far, very far, from that detested duplicity, or any of its hateful train. I never expressed an idea of you or your conduct that I did not express to yourself. It was the impulse of the moment; and I feel too independent of any man's power, however much I may choose to depend upon their good opinion and friendship, to suppress my sentiments when justly founded. For many years of my life my confidence in you was unbounded. You said you loved me with all the extravagance of passion; at the same time that respect, esteem, and veneration made you express sentiments that did you honour to feel and me to follow. You certainly did not act to my brother as I would have done to yours or to any one you protected. What Mr. Pitt told you I could not tell him as a secret. You have often told me he has none from you. I do not doubt—I could not doubt—that the Duke and I were the persons on earth you wished most to serve, and yet my brother has met with the most cruel disappointments. In this, my good friend, there is no duplicity. Not even to your enemies did I express an idea that could lead them to think that I ever doubted your honour, your sincerity, or your talents as a statesman. No dark hints and half-sentences; but an open declaration of my friendship and a dependence upon yours. That your friends and that society was where we spent the happiest hours. However impolitic, I always openly declared my decided preference to those parties, and I don't doubt it but it made enemies of those that had felt and expressed very different sentiments—I know it did. But to gain one friend such as I could name, more than repaid a legion of such insipid triflers and ignorant puppies. When I wrote you my note from London I had resolved to obliterate all causes of complaint, and only remember with gratitude the pleasant parties we had enjoyed at your house; but your letter makes it necessary that I bring to your view from how many different sources any dissatisfaction on my part arose. The last cause—your conduct relative to our politics—I thought both impolitic as a statesman and unkind as a friend. You say you thought otherwise, and your kind proposal of the Duke's succeeding to Lord Marchmont's office will more than cancel his disappointment. This is a true picture of my mind. After eighteen years' acquaintance, you would have drawn a much more flattering one; indeed, till the last few months of my life, you certainly thought me all perfection—so no more duplicity, or I must attribute eighteen years of that most horrid vice to you, and only a few months' sincerity. So I know, whatever you may amuse yourself with writing, that it is still, and must be, your firm belief. I would not have said so much upon the subject, but I tremble for I don't know what. I had hints in London. I had forgot them, till your letter brings them with redoubled force to my remembrance. I could not believe them; for you had convinced me Mr. Pitt had some unfavourable impressions of me, and that you had removed them. For no one favour did I feel more grateful. But I shall never have done. I was happy to see all your family in Edinburgh well and happy; I found my little boy the most lovely creature I ever saw. My Duke is most sincerely yours; he cannot doubt your friendship, as that office had long been the object of his wishes and expectations. No one is better entitled and no one more worthy of it. Once more adieu. May the races afford you much amusement, and may the paths of Melville and Duneira be strewed with roses, without one care from public or private life to cause a gloom.

&c., &c.,

"J. Gordon."

The Duchess, in enclosing this correspondence, begs Wilberforce to be her defender if he hears her character attacked on the ground of "duplicity" or "inaccuracy;" his influence with Pitt was one reason for her troubling him with the subject.

Later on she writes to Wilberforce, who was

gradually withdrawing himself from fashionable society, a note docketed "before 1800," to say :—

"Am I never to see you more? The Duchess of Leeds and her sister sing here Monday evening. Pray come; I shall be delighted to see you, and much mortified if you don't come.

"Ever yours most truly, &c.,

"J. GORDON."

After 1800 Wilberforce seems in great measure to have cut himself loose from society that he considered frivolous; and to have used the extraordinary influence he possessed over his friends to endeavour to induce them also to forsake the world of fashion. The long letter which follows is from Lord Calthorpe (a relation of Barbara,[1] Wilberforce's wife), who had been strongly advised by Wilberforce not to spend a Sunday with the Duchess of Gordon in Scotland. Lord Calthorpe writes in great chagrin at having neglected the good advice of his mentor, had found the warnings against her fascinations very necessary, and had had the mortification of seeing her go to sleep while he read Leighton's "Commentary" to

---

[1] William Wilberforce married Barbara, daughter of Isaac Spooner; she was the seventh Barbara in her family, the name having been handed down from mother to daughter. The first Barbara was daughter of Viscount Fauconberg and wife of Sir Henry Slingsby, Bart., who was beheaded on Tower Hill June 8, 1658, by Oliver Cromwell, for loyalty.

her. It would be of interest to know what were the "full and useful directions for public speaking" for which Lord Calthorpe is grateful to Wilberforce.

Lord Calthorpe to Mr. Wilberforce.

"KINRARA,
"*September 2, 1801, Saturday.*

"MY DEAR SIR,—I have just evinced a proof of want of vigilance and self-discipline which vexes me so much that I am endeavouring to find relief from my vexation by telling it to you, as it is a satisfaction to me to think that you will pity me, in spite of the neglect of your advice, which I have betrayed. After having had the carriage at the door to leave this place (the Duchess of Gordon's) in order that we might spend to-morrow quietly, about twenty miles off, I have suffered myself to be persuaded to stay here till Monday. O how subtle are the devices of the enemy of our peace, and how weak our natural means of defence; the real cause of my falling into this temptation is now plain enough, but the shadow of delusion that for a moment imposed upon me was the idea of having some serious conversation with the Duchess, when we were likely to be almost alone, and which company has hitherto given me but little opportunity for; and this I was weak enough to indulge in spite of more sober convictions and the advice of Mr. Gorham and other objections, and I am just awakened to see the extent of my folly, conceit, and wilful depravity, by finding that we are to have no chance of having my imagination gratified, as Sir Wm. Scott has written word that he is coming to-morrow, and the delight with which the Duchess welcomed the intelligence has opened my eyes to my sottishness in thinking her sincere in her wish that I might pass a Sunday with her. I cannot conceive a scene more calculated to excite feelings of devotion and to expose worldly vanities than this spot, which is quite lovely, yet here I have found how strongly the world may engage the affections; there is something in the Duchess that pleases, although against the judgment (perhaps a little in the way of Falstaff), and makes her entertaining even when she is the subject of melancholy reflections; indeed, I feel how necessary your warnings against her fascinations were; she talked a great deal about her friend Wilberforce, and threatens you with a letter about me, and told me all my faults which she intended to report to you; I have not spent a Sunday (for it is now over) with so much self-reproach since I came into Scotland. She seems to be on the same kind of terms with religion as she is with her Duke, that is, on terms of great nominal familiarity without ever meeting each other except in an hotel or in the streets of Edinburgh. She fell asleep on Sunday while I was reading to her part of Leighton's Commentary and awoke with lively expressions of admiration at what she had not heard; she talks of setting off for Ireland in a few weeks and of going to London afterwards, so I hope that she will do no harm at Edinburgh next winter. I left Kinrara on Monday and got to Blair at night; I found there more of ancient stateliness than I have yet seen, and I think the Duke of Athol is fond of keeping it up; he has some very fine scenery about him there, and his other place Dunkeld, which is twenty miles off, is perhaps more beautiful although less wild and magnificent. Sir W. Scott (whom I never see without thinking of you) is on a visiting tour, and went from Blair with Lord Frederick Campbell to Lord Melville's and from thence goes to the Duke of Argyle's and Montrose's back to Edinburgh; he was very tortuous and amusing. I have written this by scraps, and am ashamed to have been so long about it. Many thanks for your last letter, and especially for your kindness in giving me such full and useful directions for acquiring a talent for public speaking; I will endeavour, as far as I am able, to do justice to them, and I expect to find your technical lines of great service to me. I believe that the plan of religious reading which you mention is the best, and surely I have no small encouragement to pursue it, and when I am so great a gainer by its beneficial effects in your case.

I spent yesterday at Lord Mansfield's, at Scoone, where the Kings of Scotland used to be crowned; the old palace has been pulled down, and a very large Gothic house built upon its site. I hope you are enjoying health and quiet where you are, and every other blessing. Give my kindest remembrance to Mrs. W.

"Believe me, my dear sir,

"Affectly yours,

"CALTHORPE.

"You shall hear from me again."

Wilberforce's influence with Pitt was also known to Maria, Duchess of Gloucester.[1] It will be remembered that Henry William, third son of George II. (created Duke of Gloucester in 1764), married Maria, Dowager Countess of Waldegrave, in 1766. This lady writes to Wilberforce, hoping that through his "mediation with Pitt" a regiment of dragoons may be given to her son Lord Waldegrave.

The Duchess of Gloucester to Mr. Wilberforce.

"GENOA, *February* 4, 1786.

"SIR,—Although you did not succeed in one of my requests to Mr. Pitt, you were more successful in the other, and for that I return you my thanks. I did not very much flatter myself that Mr. Pitt would add a place to what Lord Waldegrave at

[1] She was second daughter of Sir Edward Walpole; her uncle Horace Walpole writes of her: "For beauty I think she is the first match in England, she has infinite wit and vivacity."

present possesses, indeed a regiment is almost the only addition he is likely to gain; and as Mr. Pitt has expressed his satisfaction in the marks of favour already received from the King, may I hope, through your mediation, that Mr. Pitt will be so good as to remind His Majesty how very acceptable a regiment of dragoons will be to Lord Waldegrave. If Lord Waldegrave was distressed from his own extravagance I would not trouble Mr. Pitt, but my daughter's father left his brother a clear estate which is now encumbered as much as if the late Lord Waldegrave had come to the title and estate, at twenty-four, instead of forty-four. The Duke of Grafton's reconciliation with his son is now so old a story that I only mention it as a fact that I am sensible gives you pleasure? Mr. Pitt is so much attached to Lord Euston, that I must take part in an event that I know gives him so much pleasure. I hope Lord Lucan will suffer the match to take place, but till it is over I shall have my doubts. If Mrs. Wilberforce and your sister are in town will you give them my best compliments. Sophia and William are both as tall as yourself.

"Sir,

"I remain yours, &c., &c.,

"MARIA."

The next letter is from the same lady, thanking

Wilberforce for having written "so full an explanation of what so few people understand" in his work on "Practical Christianity."

"GLOUCESTER HOUSE,
"*April* 14, 1797.

"I received your inimitable book the day before I got your letter, and had read a good way in it. I have continued to read in it with the greatest satisfaction, and beg of you to accept of my thanks for having written so full an explanation of what so few people understand. I hope and trust it will be universally read, and that with attention, as then the good it will do will be infinite. Mrs. H. More was with me last night; she is so exalted by your book that she almost forgets humility is one of the Christian requisites.

"I remain, dear sir,

"Your *very* much obliged, &c.,

"MARIA."

Let us turn to the more serious friendships of Wilberforce's middle age. So much of his correspondence with Hannah More has been published that it is only lightly touched on here.

In 1809 Hannah More wrote to Mr. Wilberforce: "Oh, if I could have had the benefit of your assistance in Cœlebs![1] but I could not be

[1] "Cœlebs in Search of a Wife," published 1809. Of her publishing experiences, Hannah More writes: "One effect of Cœlebs has pleased me. I always consider a bookseller in respect

such an unfeeling brute as to ask it. 'Tis not to *make a speech* when I say that *you* are the *only being* whose counsels would *in all points* have exactly fallen in with my own ideas from your uniting a critical knowledge of the world in its higher classes with such deep religious feelings—either of these I might have found in a very few, but not both in any."

Hannah More and her friends had apparently unfortunate experiences with regard to the spiritual help to be obtained from the higher ranks of the clergy at that time, as she writes: "I have had many interviews with Ladies Waldegrave and Euston. They told me that, though acquainted with several bishops, they never could get a word of seriousness or profit from any of them." Whether it was the "critical knowledge of the world in its higher classes" joined to "deep religious feeling" mentioned by Hannah More, or the "indulgent benevolent temper, with no pretension to superior sanctity or strictness," of which Maria Edgeworth writes,[1] certain it is that

---

to a book as I do an undertaker with regard to death—one considers a publication as the other does a corpse, as a thing to grow rich by, but not to be affected with. Davies (Cadell's partner) seems deeply struck, and earnestly implores me to follow up some of the hints respecting Scripture in a work of which he suggests the subject."

[1] "Life and Letters of Maria Edgeworth," by Augustus J. C. Hare.

Wilberforce became a guide of the religious life of many of his friends. For instance, Mr. Eliot, the brother-in-law of Pitt, writes from Burton Pynsent a letter, marked "very pleasing and serious" by Wilberforce, in which he says in answer to Wilberforce, who "hoped he had been going on in a regular, steady way," that he had been "endeavouring to work a good will into a good habit, that so the habit may come in turn to the assistance of the will, which, as you very truly say, I am sure (except under the special favour of God's grace), will flag and waver in its best pursuits and firmest intention. My chief reading for the month has been Warburton."

Mrs. Elizabeth Fry writes to Wilberforce to say:—

"When thou hast leisure, advise with me as with a child if thou hast any hint to give me in my new circumstances. I look before long once more to entering the prisons. The cause is near my heart, and I do not see that my husband, having lost his property, should, when he and my family do not want me, prevent my yet attending to these duties; in this I should like to have thy advice."

In 1801 the question of Irish Union divided educated opinion. Dr. Burgh,[1] a well-known man

[1] "Poor Burgh almost mad about the Union" ("Life of Wilberforce," vol. ii. p. 359).

at this time and friend of Wilberforce, takes one side, and Lord Hardwicke, Viceroy of Ireland, the other.

Dr. Burgh to Mr. Wilberforce.

"YORK, *February* 9, 1801.

"MY DEAR WILBER.,—I sincerely thank you for the communication you have made to me, and assure you that you may rely upon my profoundest silence. The cruel and corrupt means that were adequately resorted to, in order to effect the revolutionary Union which has subverted the prescriptive constitution of both these kingdoms, have so entirely infected the sweetness of affiance in my bosom, that whatever systems or changes are adopted my eye sets instantly to search among all possible motives in order to find the worst of issues. Can I see Addington climb upon the stooping neck of Mr. Pitt, and not believe that it is done in hostility, or in a masked confederacy? If the former, how am I to estimate the man who comes in? If the latter, what judgment can I form of the man who goes out? Is a retiring administration to be allowed, in a temporary agreement with opposition, to support the claims of Irish Popery, and by carrying their point in their new character, to exonerate the Cabinet of the charge; and are they to re-occupy their posts when there are no farther measures to be carried by them in their unresponsible situations? All this I foresaw, though not perhaps in the detail; and, indeed, it required no prophet's eye to foresee it, when hints which bind not were conscientiously substituted for promises in order to purchase a momentary calm. The downfall of the Church of England is still involved, and however the Papists of Ireland, on merging the two kingdoms into each other, may be considered as outnumbered by the Protestants, it is not by the Protestants of the Establishment, who will, on the whole, be outweighed by the incorporated force of the Protestant Dissenters with those of the same description in Ireland, who will derive the most unqualified assistance from the Romish body. Show favour to Popery, and the Dissenters' claims will be abetted by millions who will only infer a kind of right against all anticipation of consequences; or, on the other hand, deny the demands of Popery, and you instantly and directly unite the two denominations against the Church of England. I know but one mode to prevent all these, and ten thousand other unconsidered evils; at once declare the impracticability of carrying conditions into execution, and dissolve this ill-starred Union, from which no benefit will ever flow, but every evil that imagination can picture.

"I will trouble you no farther now except to

desire that you will not charge me with defective candour; the things that are already done will surely too clearly justify whatever inference I have drawn from them.

"May every happiness attend you and yours—in opposition to prospects I say it; but if a few good men may not save a nation, they yet may save and purchase favour to themselves.

"I am ever, my dear Wilber.,

"Most fervently yours,

"W. B."

Lord Hardwicke to Mr. Wilberforce.

"*September* 30, 1801.

"I think the alterations made by the Union are in some respects likely to facilitate the conduct of public business in this country with a view to the public benefit. I have hitherto had great reason to be satisfied with my reception. The city of Dublin, I mean the leading part of it, is extremely loyal and attached to Government, but they still consider the Union as having affected in some degree their local interests, and it will be some time before this feeling is entirely removed. There can however be little doubt that when they see the United Parliament as attentive to Irish as they have been to British interests, and disposed to promote them by the same liberal encouragement, that whatever partial dissatisfaction may remain will gradually wear off. If the French do not succeed in landing a considerable body of troops in this country we shall certainly continue to enjoy tranquillity, but if the enemy effect a landing in force, we must expect rebellion to revive."

The state of Ireland at a later date after the Union is alluded to in the next letter from Lord Redesdale,[1] who was apparently much aggrieved at the treatment which he had experienced in giving up the Lord Chancellorship of that country. The letter is marked by Wilberforce "Lord Redesdale shamefully used on being turned out of Chancellorship."

Lord Redesdale to Mr. Wilberforce.

"ELY PLACE, DUBLIN,
"*March* 5, 1806.

"MY DEAR SIR,—I rely upon your letter, desiring to know whether there was any establishment in this country by contribution to which you could forward its civilisation, for excusing my sending you 'observations on the necessity of publishing the Scriptures in the Irish language,' by Dr. Stokes, of the College, who is engaged in such a work, without any view of emolument, but merely to promote the civilisation of the

[1] Lord Redesdale was appointed Lord High Chancellor of Ireland March 15, 1802; he resigned February, 1806.

country, and the propagation, as much as possible, of the Christian religion in its purity. He is supported by contribution of the college, and some private contributions; but such is the temper of the Irish that even their charities, liberal as they frequently are, are more the result of pride and vanity than of any of the true feelings of the charitable mind. I think Dr. Stokes's work will be very useful; and that in spite of all the arts of the priests, the circulation of the Scriptures will prevail amongst the lower orders, and must reform even the Irish Catholic Church, which I take to be the most corrupt now remaining of all the members of the Church of Rome. It will also have the effect of enabling the Protestant clergy of the Establishment to perform their duty; namely, to endeavour to instruct those who do not understand the English language; and I think it will also enable the gentlemen of the country to gain so much of the Irish language as will give them some intercourse with their poor neighbours, where the English language is not spoken; and I think it will also contribute to diffuse the English language, which I think is a most important advantage. I have thought it my duty to subscribe ten guineas for the encouragement of Dr. Stokes, and I believe a few subscriptions with what the College proposes to give him, will encourage him to proceed with activity; as I have strong assurances that he seeks for nothing but indemnity and desires no compensation for his time or his labour. I yesterday gave up the Great Seal, in consequence of Lord Spencer's having thought fit to advise His Majesty, after he had signed a warrant for Mr. Ponsonby's appointment, to sign another for putting the Great Seal in commission, and then to send it *by express*, directing the Lord Lieutenant to *lose no time* in procuring the Commission to pass the Seal. This has been done in so much hurry that I have great doubts of its regularity; and if it had been the case of any man but myself, I should have refused to put the Great Seal to the patent, without further consideration; and I find the Lords Commissioners are very much puzzled how to act. But this I feel principally as a marked and gross personal affront to me, and through me to the Lord Lieutenant.

"I could do nothing (without the Lord Lieutenant's warrant) but despatch the business of the Court of Chancery; and yet I am not to be trusted with the Great Seal *for a few days* till the arrival of Mr. Ponsonby for that purpose; and the suitors of the Court of Chancery were to be equally injured; for the Commissioners being the Chief Justice and Chief Baron, who have too much business in their own courts to sit in the Court of Chancery, and the Master of the Rolls who cannot (from the state of his health) do more business than he does as Master of the Rolls, very little of the business which would have been dispatched by me can be done till the arrival of Mr. Ponsonby; and by that time all the counsel will be gone the circuit. I must confess I resent this wanton and childish insult (for I have no doubt the affront was intended by Lord Spencer) much more than my removal from my office, and nothing could be more insulting than the terms of the letters written by my old friend C. W. Wynne, by order of Lord Spencer, with the directions to have the patent to the Commissioners sealed forthwith. From Lord Spencer and from Wynne I had certainly a claim at least to personal civility. But it is the miserable effect of party violence to blind all those who suffer themselves to be led by it. I have the satisfaction of knowing that all those persons here whose good opinion is of any value regret my removal, and have given me most affectionate testimonies of their regard. I am sorry to add that the conduct of His Majesty's ministers, in various instances, has raised in the Protestant inhabitants of this country great and serious alarm. The expressions of Mr. Fox on the subject of the Union have sunk deep into their minds; and though it has been contrived to quiet those adverse to the Union for the moment, with a view to prevent alarm, the poison is working in their minds, and you will probably soon perceive its effects. Mr. Fox's answer to Lord Shrewsbury and Mr. Scully, as stated in the papers, has also had a very unfortunate effect. It is a libel on the Government of the country in all its parts; imputing to it gross partiality even in the administration of justice, and it promises the Roman Catholics a different order of things; not by the interposition of the legislature, but *by the influence and favour of the executive* government; and it applies itself directly and particularly to the *army*, as if it were intended to frighten the Protestants into acquiescence. It should be recollected that Lord Shrewsbury is not connected in any way with Ireland, except by a claim of peerage; and that Mr. Scully is the author of a pamphlet in which he writes of James the Second as *the lawful King of Ireland* at the battle of the Boyne, and King William as a *Dutch invader*. You can have no conception of the gloom which prevails in the minds of thinking people in this country. Our Chief Justice and Chief Baron, both very sound men and highly esteemed, are very strongly affected. The Chief Justice forebodes every species of mischief. Lord Norbury, who is Chief Justice of the Common Pleas, is of a lighter turn of mind, and irritated by a gross and ridiculous affront in omitting his name in the Commission for custody of the Great Seal—evidently a mere piece of party malice. But he also is full of gloomy apprehensions of the result of the measures likely to be adopted.

"But my apprehensions are greatly increased by observing that Lord Grenville and Lord Spencer are mere dupes to the other party in the Cabinet with respect to Ireland, if not generally so. Lord Grenville and Lord Spencer perhaps imagine that they may have some influence in Ireland through Mr. Elliott and Sir J. Newport. Most certainly they will have none. The Ponsonby family will govern Ireland through the Lord Lieutenant, who is completely in their hands. Lord Grenville and Lord Spencer seem also to have put Scotland and India out of their control; and with the influence of all the great appendages of the Empire against them, and a majority in the Cabinet to contend with at home, what can they hope for? As the least of two evils, I shall yet feel it my duty to support them against their rivals in the Cabinet, though the personal insults I have received have come through them, and their rivals have been comparatively civil. I shall get rid of my property here as soon as I can, and with the miserable remains transport myself to England for the rest of my days.

"I have had enough of office, and especially in my last change, which has had the effect of making me pay a fine of at least twenty thousand pounds for the honour of serving four years in a laborious office, separated from my family and all my old friends. I shall return to England, however, with pleasure; for though I shall be reduced to practise an economy to which for thirty years I have been a stranger, I shall return to my old friends, and to a country where my life will probably be in no greater danger than that of any other person, and where Lady Redesdale will be relieved from the fear and anxieties which have long agitated her mind, and made her ardently wish that I had never taken the office of Chancellor of Ireland; a wish in which I most heartily concur. The remainder of my life I trust will be passed more quietly than the last three years. Lady Redesdale begs to join in respects to Mrs. Wilberforce, and I am

"Truly, my dear sir,

"Your faithful, humble servant,

"REDESDALE."

Sydney Smith writes in 1807 with regard to the Yorkshire election, and the state of

Ireland: his letter is marked "characteristic" by Wilberforce.

"DEAR SIR,—If Mrs. S. remains in her present state of health I hardly know how I can go down to Yorkshire at all. It is eight weeks since her lying-in, and she cannot yet stand upon her feet. If I do come I will certainly vote for Lord Milton and for you. I hope now you have done with Africa you will do something for Ireland, which is surely the greatest question and interest connected with this Empire. There is no man in England who from activity, understanding, character, and neutrality could do it so effectually as Mr. Wilberforce—and when this country conceded a century ago an establishment to the Presbyterian Church, it is horrible to see four millions of Christians of another persuasion instructed by ragged priests, and praising their Creator in wet ditches. I hope to God you will stir in this great business, and then we will vote you the consulship for life, and you shall be perpetual member for Yorkshire.

"In the meantime I remain, with great respect,

"Your obedient servant,

"SYDNEY SMITH."

Wilberforce had evidently written to Lord Eldon begging him not to take up the great question of abolition of slavery on party grounds; and Lord

Eldon wrote that he wished that the House of Lords might not disgrace itself by its mode of proceeding, as he saw a strong inclination to do justice, "if abolition be justice, in a most unjust mode." This letter is undated; it was probably written in 1802.

Lord Eldon to Mr. Wilberforce.

"DEAR SIR,—I thank you for your book, and I add my thanks for your letter. You may be assured that I am incapable of 'taking up this great question on party grounds.' As a proof of that, I may mention that after listening more than once, with the partiality which my love of his virtues created, to Mr. Pitt himself in the House of Commons, and discussing the subject with him in private, again and again, the difficulties which I had upon immediate abolition, and abolition without compensation previously pledged (not compensation for British debts out of African blood, but out of British treasure) never were so far surmounted, as to induce me to think I had clear grounds for voting *with him*. After such a statement, I need not say that, although my political life has, at least so I fancy, for near twenty-four years been so far really regulated by a sincere belief that I am acting according to the dictates of duty in an uniform uninterrupted opposition to some persons now in power, that I feel it very difficult to class among my honourable friends gentlemen who have never, that I know of, disavowed the principles against which I have been waging war, and who, I presume, have never disavowed them because they entertained them, as sincerely as I detest them; yet, in a case of this sort, I know that I must either stand or fall by taking diligent heed that in what I do or forbear to do I am governed by the best lights, which my own reason, aided by information, can afford me; and I should think myself a worse man, if I was influenced by party considerations in such a business, than indiscreet zeal has yet represented a West India planter to be.

"What I shall finally do I know not. I wish the House of Lords may not disgrace itself by its mode of proceeding. I see or think I see a strong inclination, if abolition be justice, to do justice in a most unjust mode. Perhaps the dilatory conduct of that House formerly, it is now thought, can be atoned for by hurry and precipitation. And that its character will be best maintained by its being doubly disgraced. I wish my mind had been so framed as to feel no doubts on this awful and fearful business, but as that is not the case, I must endeavour to do as rightly as, with my infirmities of mind I may be able to act. I shall see to-day what course the matters take, and if my view of the subject leads me to determine to vote and I feel it likely to be beneficial to converse upon facts, as well as to read all I can find, I shall seek the benefit you kindly offer me.

"Yours sincerely,

"ELDON."

Wilberforce had met Lord Ellenborough on the Continent in 1785, and had maintained a friendly intercourse with him. The following letter from Lord Ellenborough shows his attitude towards abolition. Though he acknowledged the viciousness of the system he was extremely alarmed at the consequences of disturbing it (especially in the then convulsed state of the world). At the same time he said that he should not be governed by any supposed policy of man, if he were clear as to the will of God on the point. His letter is marked "truly pleasing" by Wilberforce.

Lord Ellenborough to Mr. Wilberforce.

"BLOOMSBURY SQUARE,

"*June* 27, 1802.

"MY DEAR SIR,—I recollect perfectly the conversation between us in the House of Commons to which you allude, and should be extreme happy to appoint a time when I might have the benefit, which I should certainly derive from a communication with you upon the important subject mentioned in your letter,—if I could do so with convenience to you, and without breaking in upon my necessary attendance during the sittings at Westminster and Guildhall—and which occupy me from half-past eight to four or later every day—and on some days I am afterwards obliged to attend the House of Lords till between five and six. If there be any morning this week during which my sittings will continue at Westminster, when it might be convenient to you to be at my chamber at Westminster, called the King's Bench Treasury Chamber, by half-past eight, I would be down there by that time, which would allow me the satisfaction of seeing you for half hour before my sittings, which commence at nine, begin. I feel the infinite importance of the question of abolition, and will give no vote upon it at all, unless I can do so with a much more satisfied judgment and conscience on the subject than I have attained at present. I have always felt a great abhorrence of the mode by which these unfortunate creatures are torn from their families and country, and have doubted whether any sound policy could grow out of a system which seemed to be so vicious in its foundation; but I am extremely alarmed at the consequences of disturbing it, particularly in the present convulsed state of the world. In short, my dear sir, I am almost ashamed to say that I tremble at giving their full effect to the impressions which the subject naturally makes on my mind, in the first view of it, as a man and a Christian. I am frightened at the consequences of any innovation upon a long-established practice, at a period so full of danger as the present. At the same time I cannot well reconcile it with the will of God,—and if I was quite clear on that head, I should be decided by it, and should not be governed by any supposed policy of man which might be set up in opposition to it. I write this in confidence to yourself. I remain, my dear sir, with very sincere respect,

"Your obedient servant,

"ELLENBOROUGH."

Wilberforce had written to Lord Ellenborough on the evils of his having a seat in the Cabinet, Lord Ellenborough being at that time Lord Chief Justice of the King's Bench, and the next letter contains Lord Ellenborough's defence of his conduct, which does not err on the side of brevity and which Wilberforce describes as "a very handsome answer."

Lord Ellenborough to Mr. Wilberforce.

"BLOOMSBURY SQUARE,
"*February* 4, 1806.

"MY DEAR SIR,—I sit down to thank you for the favour of your letter in the very instant in which I have received it. I regret very much that I have no opportunity of personal communication with you on the subject of it: if I had I could explain more perfectly and unreservedly than I can do by letter all the motives which have induced my reluctant acquiescence in a nomination of myself to a place in the

Cabinet. The situation has not only not been sought by me, but I appeal to every member of the Government about to be formed who is acquainted with the transaction, whether it was not accepted by me with extreme reluctance, and after objections raised by myself which nothing but a superior sense of the present duty and a prospect of present usefulness to the public would have surmounted. If I had felt that a situation in the Cabinet would have placed me under circumstances inconsistent with the due and impartial discharge of my judicial functions, no consideration on earth would have induced me to accept it. A member of the Cabinet is only a member of a Select Committee of the Privy Council, of which Privy Council at large every justice of the K. B. is of course a member. In that larger Privy Council his Majesty may and frequently does take the opinion of its members on matters which may come in question judicially before some of them. But I think that no man can correctly act in both capacities, and therefore when a question of a high criminal nature was about a year ago under discussion at a Privy Council at which I was particularly desired by the Chancellor to attend, I stipulated expressly with my Lord Chancellor that I should not be included in a Special Commission to try the offence then under consideration. I think both my Lord C. J. Holt, and very lately my Lord C. J. Eyre would have done better to have forborne being present at the preliminary inquiries before the Privy Council, the subjects of which in the result might be, and afterwards in fact were, tried before them; but the objection is not so much in my opinion that I might be led to participate in the counsels of the Executive Government upon questions connected with the criminal jurisdiction which I am to exercise elsewhere (because from these I should of course invariably withdraw myself) but because it might give a political cast and bias to a judicial mind, might generate views of ambition, and destroy that indifference and impartiality on all questions which is the proper characteristic of a British judge, and even if it had not that effect, it might be supposed by the world at large to produce it, which very opinion of others would detract much from the public credit and consequent usefulness of the person so circumstanced.

"The consideration of this objection at first gave my mind no small degree of anxiety. I was conscious to myself that I had no views of ambition to gratify. Those views, if I had entertained any such, would have been better consulted by accepting the Great Seal, and with it a highly efficient place in the public Councils—but which I had already refused—indeed every view of that kind has been long since more than satisfied. I lent myself at the earnest solicita tion of others to the great public object of forming a strong and united administration, which, perhaps, without my consent to accept this situation could not, from particular circumstances and difficulties which I am not at liberty to state, have been formed.

"In accepting it I have stipulated that I should not be expected to attend except on particularly important occasions, and on such occasions some of my predecessors and particularly Lord Mansfield has, I understand, been called upon for his advice, and indeed, in virtue of my oath as Privy Councillor I am bound to give that advice when required.

"Will you acquit me of vanity?—I hope you will, when I give one reason more for my consenting to become for a time (I hope it will be a short one) an ostensible member of his Majesty's select and confidential Council. As I had, so I hoped I should be understood to have, no motive of ambition or interest inducing me to take this place in his Majesty's Councils. I had in general been supposed on most subjects to think for myself. I had, I believe, been considered in general as a zealous friend to the just prerogatives of the Crown. I had no particular stain upon my private character: in the miscellaneous composition of every administration, and of this, amongst others, I thought a person such as I might be esteemed to be, and on the ground of that estimation particularly, would be an ingredient not wholly without its use.

"So it appeared to some of my friends. So it did (I speak it in confidence) particularly to Lord Sidmouth, as to the purity of whose views and conduct in the formation of the present arrangement I can bear the fullest testimony, and whose earnest request (I speak it still in the same confidence) overcame my reluctance, and induced me to make this sacrifice of private convenience and to incur the hazard which your kind and honourable letter represents to me as greater than I had thought it, of suffering in the good opinion of others. If, after this explanation, unavoidably less perfect than I could have wished to make it, you shall still retain your unfavourable opinion of the step I have taken, I shall learn it from you (and I am sure in that case you will have the frankness to tell me so) with inexpressible pain. As long as I shall continue a member of his Majesty's Councils (and I hope the necessity which induced my acceptance of the situation will not be of long continuance) I will give a faithful, honest, and fearless opinion upon the subjects under consideration, and, although it is possible that good men may doubt of the prudence or propriety of my conduct in accepting it, I am confident that no good man who shall have the means of knowing the actual course I shall pursue in that situation will have reason to blame it. The explanation I have given you is entirely confidential. With an anxious wish consistently to perform all the various duties which press upon me at this moment and to preserve the good opinion of good men, and especially of one whom on many accounts I have so long and so highly esteemed as yourself,

"I remain, my dear sir,

"Most sincerely and faithfully yours,

"ELLENBOROUGH."

In 1802, on the supposition that Lord Wellesley's resignation as Governor-General of India was imminent, an idea had been entertained that Lord Castlereagh should be offered the Governor-Generalship, and Wilberforce had been asked to approach him on the subject. From Lord Camden's letter to Wilberforce, given below, it will be seen that Pitt had objected to an appointment that would take Lord Castlereagh from the House of Commons, which he thought should be the theatre of his future fame.

Lord Camden to Mr. Wilberforce.

"*January* 7, 1802.

"DEAR WILBERFORCE,—I lament extremely that Lady Camden and I have been deprived of the pleasure we should have had in receiving you and Mrs. Wilberforce here, and still more that you should have been confined to London by the very anxious attendance you have undergone. I thank you for communicating with me on the subject of Lord Castlereagh, and I will explain to you all I know of his objects as connected with the situation you have mentioned.

"Amongst the many unpleasant circumstances attending our secession from office I have considered Lord Castlereagh's actual situation as one peculiarly awkward to himself, and I have also thought that in the present dearth of men of spirit and sense who *can* take office it was unfortunate for the country that he should be excluded. With a view of relieving him, if possible, from such exclusion, I contrived that he should meet Pitt here about a month ago, and have a full and explicit conversation with him and me relative to the future views of the one and the future prospects of the other. (I confess I was not indifferent at the same time to the consideration of the line I may myself hereafter think it right to adopt.) In a previous conversation I had with Pitt respecting Lord Castlereagh, he expressed his anxiety that he should take office, and he is desirous of contriving it if possible with credit to him; and amongst the objects to which Lord Castlereagh might look, he took notice to me of an idea which he knew had been entertained of sending him to the East Indies as Governor-General. He (Pitt), however, expressed an objection to this appointment, as it would take him from the House of Commons, which *he* thought should be the theatre of his future fame, and where, whenever Lord Hawkesbury is removed, he will be much wanted. In preparing Lord Castlereagh for his conversation with Pitt I mentioned to him the idea which had been entertained of his going to India, but I took notice of it as a mere floating idea that had not been matured, and in the short conversation upon that part of the subject which ensued, his impression appeared to be an unwillingness to banish himself from his country and to withdraw for ever (as he should conceive he did, by now abandoning it) from the situation he had a right to look for in the House of Commons. In the subsequent conversation with Pitt at which I was present, not a word passed on this subject, and I should therefore conceive that Lord Castlereagh has never had the subject fairly before him. I am convinced he would have communicated with me if he had; and although I should conceive it very doubtful if the event might turn out as you wish, if the proposition were made to him, I yet think if the directors of the East India Company have really thought of him, he ought to have the opportunity of weighing a subject of this great importance in his mind before he has been understood to decline the offer. By way of apprising Lord

Castlereagh upon the subject I will enclose him your letter (if you have no objection), which I think will give him the opinion of a person indifferent to everything concerning him except his public character, and open the business in as advantageous a manner as it can be done.

"Believe me,

"Ever most sincerely yours,

"CAMDEN."

In 1803 the tardiness of our military preparations had been accentuated in a debate on the second reading of the Army Reserve Bill. Windham, of whom Wilberforce says that "he had many of the true characteristics of a hero, but he had one great fault as a statesman, he hated the popular side of any question," gives as his opinion in the next letter, that he saw no impossibility in two armies of from twenty to thirty thousand men being landed in different places, and being opposed only by yeomanry and volunteers they might advance to London or wherever else they pleased. "Government acknowledge that there is an utter want of firearms."[1] Windham's hope was that Buonaparte might, for some reason or other, not come; though he confesses that he did not know of any foundation for such hope.

[1] Wilberforce to Henry Bankes. "Life of W. Wilberforce," vol. iii. p. 117.

Right Hon. William Windham to Mr. Wilberforce.
"BEACONSFIELD,
"*August* 18, 1803.

"DEAR WILBERFORCE,— The breaking up of Parliament, advanced as the season is, I can hardly help regretting on another account. One wants a means of publishing the abominable backwardness in which things are with respect to defence: so as literally to put us in the situation, described by some writer in the *Moniteur*, namely that if fifty thousand men can anyhow get on shore, they must conquer the island. What shall we say to the fact, that at the end of now more than five months since the King's message not a single ball cartridge (I suppose) has been fired from one end of the country to the other, unless perhaps a few that I have desired to be fired just by me in Norfolk, and some that I hear Grey has been using upon the same principle in Northumberland?—that the corps, which have been raising, such as they are, remain to this moment for the greater part without arms?—that excepting, I am afraid, a very few thousand men to the army of reserve, not the smallest addition has been or can be made to a force truly regular, such as can alone be opposed upon equal terms to the troops by which we shall be invaded?—and that the whole assistance, that would be to be received from works, of whatever sort, is all yet to be begun, and even settled? When men talk of the difficulties and impracticability of invasion, of the impossibility of conquering a country such as this, they say what may be true, but which is certainly not so for any reasons which they can, or at least which they do, give. It is all a kind of loose, general vague notion founded on what they have been accustomed to see and to conceive, to which the answer is that so was everything which we have seen successively happen for these last fourteen years. Considering things not in much detail, but upon principles somewhat less general than those which I have been alluding to, I can see no impossibility in the supposition of two armies landing in different places of from twenty to thirty thousand men each, of their beating, severally, the troops immediately opposed to them, and that having nothing then to encounter but volunteers and yeomanry, and other troops of this description, in the midst of all the confusion and panick which would then prevail, that they might advance to London or wherever else they pleased. What the further consequences might be, one has no pleasure in attempting to trace; but I should be obliged to any one who would show me some distinct limits to them. The persons to do this are, I am sure, not those who talk so glibly of crushing and overwhelming, and smothering, and I know not what all; without the least idea how any of these things are to be done, while the persons attacking us know how these things are, sometimes at least, not done, by the example of the numerous countries which they have overrun in spite of all such threatened opposition. I shall go from here, that is from London, as soon as I have settled some necessary business, and see whether I can be of any use in Norfolk, though I do not perceive how with the aid of only a single regiment of militia (all our present force) we are to stop a body of even one thousand men, or how for the present, anything at all can be done, when there is not as yet a provision for even the delivery of arms. All the firelocks which they have as yet got immediately about here have been sent down at my own expense. My chief hopes are I confess that Buonaparte may, for some reason or another, not come, or at least for some time; but what foundation there is for any such hope I confess I do not know. Forgive my running on at this rate. The importance of the subject would certainly warrant me if I had anything new to say.

"Yours very truly,

"W. WINDHAM."

Lord Chatham[1] at that time Master-General of the Ordnance, writes on the same subject: at any rate

[1] Brother to Mr. Pitt, of whom Lord Eldon gave it as his deliberate opinion that "the ablest man I ever knew in the Cabinet was Lord Chatham."

there were "one hundred thousand pikes ready for the defence of the country, but there was an indisposition to take them."

Lord Chatham to Mr. Wilberforce.
"St. James' Square,
"*September* 2, 1803.

"I had certainly felt it my duty (as only following up the plan proposed before I came to the Ordnance) to endeavour to restore at the Peace, and with such improvements as could be suggested, the manufacture of the old Tower musquet, which our troops used to have, but which the necessities of the late war, and the naked state of our arsenals at its commencement, had obliged us to depart from, and to have recourse to an inferior arm. I found of course considerable opposition to any improvement, not only from the manufacturers, but from all the inferior servants of the Ordnance. This was, however, nearly surmounted, and the manufacture of the better sort of arm on the point of taking place, when this sudden and unprecedented demand for arms took place. I ought here to state that had it not been with a view to improvement, and intending gradually to dispose of those of inferior quality through the medium of the India Company, we should not have been, previous to the war breaking out, carrying on any manufacture of arms, our arsenals being overflowing, calculating on the most extended scale the Department had ever been called upon to furnish. I have, however, in consequence of the extraordinary calls of the present crisis, determined to use every effort to meet it, and directions have been given to the Board of Ordnance to revert to the same arm as was made last war, and to manufacture to the utmost possible extent the musquet of the India pattern. You will easily believe I must have felt some reluctance in being obliged to take this step after all the pains I have bestowed, but I hope I have judged for the best. I have great satisfaction in thinking that the stock of arms we possess will enable us in the first instance, to arm to a considerable extent perhaps all that is really useful, and as arms come in, which with the exertions of the manufacturers they will do quickly, and with the aid of what we expect from abroad the remainder will be provided before long. We have already one hundred thousand pikes, and can increase them rapidly, but in general there is an indisposition to take them. I should like much to talk over with you, not only the subject of arms, but the whole question of volunteering which I contemplate as a most serious one. Excuse great haste with which I have written, and with Lady Chatham's very best remembrances to you, " Believe me, yours very sincerely,

"CHATHAM."

Henry Bankes, the old friend of both Pitt and Wilberforce, writes on the political situation in 1807 as follows :—

Mr. Bankes to Mr. Wilberforce.
"KINGSTON HALL,
"*January* 1, 1807.

"MY DEAR WILBERFORCE,—Upon perusing the French papers I am well satisfied with the conduct of our Government. The tone is firm and uniform, and the demands such that we might have felt extremely happy to have made peace if we could have obtained them. There is somewhat of a blundering about the basis, which you will recollect Lord Malmesbury wrote so much ingenious nonsense about upon a former occasion, and it is to be lamented that Mr. Fox (whose letters upon the whole do him great honour) laid down an indistinct and indefinite basis in general terms of loose construction instead of binding that Proteus, his friend Talleyrand, to whom in his first address he professes the most perfect *attachment* (what a word from a Minister not born in the days of Charles II.!) to the sense in which he meant to interpret, fairly as I think, his words, and the words of his master.

"Nothing can equal the shabbiness, chicanery, and double dealing of the French negotiators, and their proceedings do in fact but little credit to their understandings, if they have any opinion of ours.

"Believe me, my dear Wilberforce,
"Most sincerely yours,
"Henry Bankes."

Lord Harrowby, who twice refused the Premiership, writes of the state of parties in 1809.

Lord Harrowby to Mr. Wilberforce.

"*Friday, September* 22, 1809.

"Dear Wilberforce,—You must have thought me a great bear not to have thanked you sooner for your kind recollection of my wish to see a sketch of Mrs. H. More's rustic building. It is much more finished than I wished, and shall be sent to Kensington as soon as Mrs. Ryder has taken a slight sketch of it.

"I have, since I received it, taken two journies into Devonshire, upon Maynooth business, and have not had, when in town, a spare moment from Indian and domestic torments. The history of the latter could not be put upon paper, and if it could, would be as voluminous as an Indian despatch. You know enough of the parties not to suspend your opinion till you know as much as is necessary to form it. The Duke of Portland's resignation has only accelerated the crisis, and you know enough of Perceval to be sure that we are not broken up, because *he* insists upon having the whole power in his own hands, and will not serve under any third person. Under these circumstances, and a thousand others, there seemed no resource left, but to attempt an overture to Lord Grey and Grenville jointly, which is made with the King's consent and authority. If it is met in the spirit in which it is made, I trust it will be successful. Whatever we may be *driven* to do, if they shut their ears to the proposal of an extended and combined administration, we shall not, in my opinion, have been justified in our own eyes or in those of the country, if any party feelings prevented us from *endeavouring bonâ fide* to form such a Government as may both protect the King, and be fit for these times. They are, I believe, as little able to form a separate Government as ourselves, unless they mean to re-unite themselves with those at whose proceedings they were so evidently alarmed last year. If they come in alone by force, they will have the Catholic question as a millstone round their necks. The very fact of an union with us who are known to entertain a decidedly opposite opinion upon that question (some of us for ever, and all during the King's life) would enable them to get rid of it for the present, as, without any pledge, which, after all that has passed, could neither be asked nor given, that question could never be made a Government question without the immediate dissolution of the administration.

"You express a very flattering satisfaction at my return to public life. It will probably be a very short excursion, and certainly a most painful one. I look for no comfort but in planting turnips in my Sabine farm.

"Yours ever most sincerely,

"HARROWBY."

Lord Erskine writes in 1813, to Wilberforce:—

"I cannot sufficiently discharge a duty I owe to the public without telling you what I think of the speech you sent me on the Christian question in India. The subject, though great and important, was local and temporary; but the manner in which you treated it made your speech of the greatest value in the shield of Christianity that eloquence and faith could possibly have manufactured.

"I read it with the highest admiration, and as I am now a private man for the remaining years of my life, I may say, without the presumption of station to give weight to my opinion, that it deserves a place in the library of every man of letters, even if he were an atheist, for its merit in everything that characterises an appeal to a Christian assembly on the subject of Christianity. With the greatest regard I ever am,

"My dear sir,

"Your most faithful servant,

"ERSKINE."

Rowland Hill, the celebrated preacher, the disciple of Whitefield, and the founder of the Surrey Chapel, writes to bring before Wilberforce's notice the question of "untaxed worship," with regard to his chapel.

Rev. Rowland Hill to Mr. Wilberforce.

"SURREY CHURCH,
"*April* 16, 1814.

"MY DEAR SIR,—Another prosecution for poor rates on our chapel has commenced. Though the appellant, Mr. Farquarson, a man of no character and involved in debt, is the ostensible person, yet all the evil arises from a Mr. Whitlock, who has a place in the lottery office under Government, who probably might have been quiet had he received a hint from the Government that his designs were not correspondent with their wishes. As matters are, the most vexatious and perplexing consequences must be the result. Different persons are subpœna'd down as far as Rygate, while these large expenses *a third time over* is the least of the evil that must result. If they gain a verdict, for the sake of thousands of religious people that must be ruined by such a taxation, we must and shall resist. Surely the present mild Government will not suffer us to be deprived of the privilege of untaxed worship that we have uninterruptedly so long enjoyed.

"If, dear sir, you could but hint to Mr. Vansittart what must be the result of his neglecting to answer our respectful petitions so as to obtain some redress on our behalves, thousands would have to bless you, and none more so than

"Yours most respectfully,
"ROWLAND HILL.

"It should appear according to the new French constitution that our religious liberties in England are soon likely to be much inferior to those in France.

"We humbly conceive we have some little claim on the attention of the Government against these vexatious disputes, having made the largest collection of any place of worship in the kingdom on different patriotic calls."

It will be remembered that when the Duke of Wellington was ambassador to Paris in 1814 he took up very warmly the question of the Slave Trade, himself circulating in Paris Wilberforce's letter to his Yorkshire constituents on the subject, which Madam de Staël had translated at the Duke's suggestion, and also undertaking to disperse Wilberforce's pamphlet to Talleyrand. The Duke writes from Paris, December 14, 1814.

The Duke of Wellington to Mr. Wilberforce.

"It is impossible to describe the prejudice of all classes here upon the subject, particularly those of our determined enemies, the principal officers and *employés* in the public departments. I was in hopes that the King's measures had changed the public opinion in some degree, of which the silence of the public journals appeared an evidence. But I found yesterday that I was much mistaken, and that the desire to obtain the gain expected in the trade is surpassed only by that of misrepresenting our views and measures, and depreciating the merit we have in the abolition. I was yesterday told gravely by the Directeur de la Marine that one of our objects in abolishing the Slave Trade was to get recruits to fight our battles in America! and it was hinted that a man might as well be a slave for agricultural labour as a soldier for life, and that the difference was not worth the trouble of discussing it."

The Duke goes on to complain that what was taking place in Paris as to the Slavery question had got into the English newspapers.

The Duke of Wellington to Mr. Wilberforce.

"I am quite convinced that the only mode in which the public opinion upon it here can be brought to the state in which we wish to see it, is to keep the question out of discussion in England by public bodies and by the newspapers, and I must say that it is but fair towards the King of France not to make public in England that which he has not published to his subjects. We shall do good in this question in France only in proportion as we shall anticipate and carry the public opinion with us ; and in recommending to avoid discussion at present in order to make some progress in the opinion of France, I may lay claim to the merit of sacrificing the popularity which I should have acquired by having been the instrument to prevail upon the French Government to prevent the renewal of the trade on that part of the coast on which we had effectually abolished it during the war. I see that Mr. Whitbread mentioned the subject at a public meeting in the city, which I hope will be avoided at least till the French Government will have carried into execution all it proposes to do at present.

"Ever, my dear sir, yours most faithfully,
"WELLINGTON."

The Duke of Wellington's letter to General Macaulay is on the same subject : he says that in the case of the Slave Trade he could only be successful in France by being secret. He evidently disapproves of the people "who will have news and newspapers at their breakfasts," and thinks that the great cause had suffered from prematurely published reports.

The Duke of Wellington to General Macaulay.
"PARIS, *December* 22, 1814.

"MY DEAR MACAULAY,—I received only yesterday your letter of the 9th, and I had already received one from Mr. Wilberforce on the same subject, to which I have written an answer. I am quite certain that he has nothing to say to the publication in question.

"It is, I believe, very true that secrecy in such a matter cannot be expected, but the people of England ought to advert to this circumstance when they are pushing their objects, and if they will have news and newspapers at their breakfasts they should show a little forbearance towards their Governments, if Foreign Courts are a little close towards their agents. In the case of the Slave Trade I could be successful in this country only by being secret, and in proportion as we should be secret. And in point of fact I have found the agents of this Government much more disposed lately to oppose our views than they were six weeks ago, and I have been reproached with having allowed what has been done to be published in our newspapers.

"I must observe also that though Mr. Wilberforce could not prevent what was published from appearing in the newspapers, Mr. Whitbread might have avoided to mention the subject at a public meeting held in London upon some other subject; but the truth is that we mix up our party politics with our philanthropy and everything else, and I suspect we don't much care what object succeeds or fails provided it affects the Ministers of the day.

"Matters here are apparently in the same state as when you went away, but I believe are really in a better state; the appointments of Monsieur Didule to the Police and of Marshal Soult to the War Department have done some good.

"Ever yours,
"WELLINGTON."

Wilberforce was a member of a committee for the relief of the "poor German sufferers," the wounded Prussians in 1814-15. The translation of Marshal Blucher's letter to the Managing Committee after Waterloo is as follows.[1]

"CHATILLON SUR SAMBRE,
"*June* 24, 1815.

"Are you now satisfied? In eight days I have fought two bloody battles, besides five considerable engagements. I have taken one fortress, and keep three more surrounded. Yesterday the worthy Wellington was with me: we are agreed, we go hand in hand: the blockaded fortresses will not stop our operations, and if the Austrians and Russians do not speedily push forward, we shall finish the game ourselves. Farewell, and remember me to all England.

"BLUCHER.

[1] Part of this letter only is printed in "Life of William Wilberforce."

"It is all very well, but I have twenty-two thousand killed and wounded. It is one consolation that they fell in the cause of humanity. I hope in England care will be taken of our suffering brethren; put it to the feelings of Mr. Wilberforce and other friends."

In a later letter to Wilberforce, Marshal Blucher disclaims the idea that personal affection for himself had had anything to do with the unexampled liberality of the English to his suffering fellow countrymen. For this liberality he begs to be allowed to offer other motives. 1. The flattering description by the Duke of Wellington of the conduct of the Prussians at the Battle of Waterloo; 2. The command of the Prince Regent to make collections for them in all the churches of Great Britain; and 3. Wilberforce's "own noble exertions in their behalf." He entreats Wilberforce to be the organ of his gratitude to the whole English nation.

Marshal Blucher to Mr. Wilberforce.

"BONN, *December* 7, 1815.

"SIR,—Your letter, dated the 31st of October, reached me in safety, and with it the cheering intelligence that the English nation, and all the subscribers for the relief of the Prussians who have suffered in the present war, and for the survivors of those who have fallen, have borne an honourable testimony to their lively interest in the cause, by the greatest and most unexampled liberality.

"In your letter, sir, you are so good as to say, that it is in some measure owing to the personal affection felt for me by your countrymen, that this liberality has exceeded any which in similar circumstances has ever been exhibited; and you appeal to my own experience in the support of this assertion. It is true that during my residence in England I met everywhere with the most flattering reception; and I hope I shall always remember it with gratitude. But this very recollection confirms my belief, that the imagination of my services was magnified by that affectionate goodwill which is always the result of personal intercourse. I cannot otherwise account for the attentions which I received.

"But, sir, allow me to say that other motives than those of personal goodwill to me have quickened the exertions of the British nation for the relief of the suffering Prussians. I allude to the flattering description of their conduct at the battle of Waterloo, by the most noble the Duke of Wellington, and to the command of His Royal Highness the Prince Regent, to make collections for them in all the churches of Great Britain: neither let me forget to mention as a most powerful cause your own noble exertions in their behalf.

"Allow me, sir, to present you my most cordial thanks for this fresh service which you have rendered to suffering humanity. Let me also entreat you, my truly noble friend, you, who so richly deserve the blessings of the whole human race, for having so courageously defended their rights, to be the organ of my gratitude, and to present my acknowledgments to the whole English nation for their very generous assistance to my brave companions in arms, and to the survivors of those who have fallen. May this liberality, which we cannot but receive as an undoubted proof of the truest friendship and esteem, prove a fresh bond of union between us. We fought for the highest blessings which human nature is capable of enjoying—for Liberality and Peace. May our high-spirited people be firmly united in so noble a confederacy, and may that union never be interrupted.

"Much as, at my advanced age, I cannot but feel the necessity of repose, still should it please Providence to prolong my life, I shall yet hope once more to revisit England, and to repeat my thanks for the sympathy of that generous nation.

"I entreat you to accept the assurances of my sincere esteem and high consideration; and I have the honour to remain, sir, your most devoted servant,

"BLUCHER."

Lord Holland,[1] described as "truly fascinating, having something of his uncle's good humour," by Wilberforce, writes of Abolition to him in 1815, and thinks "the cause had been very coldly supported, if not actually betrayed, at Paris, at Madrid, and at Rio Janeiro; and that we ought to have imposed conditions on this subject when Ferdinand VII. wanted money, instead of giving him the money first."

Lord Holland to Mr. Wilberforce.
"HOLLAND HOUSE,
"*November* 13, 1815.

"DEAR SIR,—I heard that you were anxious to get some paper on the Slave Trade translated into Italian. An Italian gentleman who is upon a visit to me will, I am sure, very willingly undertake it, and is well qualified for the task, as he writes his language with great elegance and understands ours. I am afraid you will not find his Holiness as much disposed to anathematise rapine and murder committed under the sanction of the powerful Crown of Spain, as to disdain the extravagances of the Catholicks in Ireland. There was no difficulty in abolishing the French Slave Trade last year but in the breasts of the Bourbons and their adherents. Bonaparte by

---

[1] The third Lord Holland was Fox's nephew, and converted his palace at Kensington into a sort of temple in honour of Fox's memory.

doing it at once lost no adherents either in France or in the colonies, and the repugnance felt in 1814 to the measure *at Court* originated from their persuasion that the principles of all Abolitionists, as well as of all toleration in religion, are more or less connected with notions of political liberty which they know to be incompatible with their system of Government. True French Royalists, and many English Royalists too, make no difference between you and me or between me and Tom Paine. We are all equally heretics in Religion and Jacobins in Politics. There is therefore nothing to be done with that class of men in the great cause of Abolition, but by fear. We have already lost many opportunities, and if we do not now insist on Portugal and Spain abandoning the trade, and on France and the other powers treating it as piracy if they do not, we shall have shifted the ignominy from ourselves, but we shall not have rescued the world from the evil. May I ask if you understand why the complete abolition in France (if that measure of Bonaparte be really and in proper form confirmed) does not make part of the treaty? It seems to me that at Paris, at Madrid, and at Rio Janeiro the cause has been very coldly, or at least very inefficiently, supported, if it has not been actually betrayed. When Ferdinand VII. wanted money we might have imposed conditions on this and on other subjects, but we gave the money first, and he now sets us at defiance. With many apologies for the length of my letter,

"I am, sir, yours truly,

"Vassall Holland."

Early in 1825, William Wilberforce's brilliant Parliamentary career came to an end by his own voluntary retirement. The Speaker's[1] letter is the expression of a very general feeling both in the House and outside it.

The Right Hon. Speaker of the House of Commons to Mr. Wilberforce.

"Palace Yard,

"*February* 19, 1825

"My dear Sir,—With respect to your quitting us for more private retirement, permit me to say with the truest sincerity, and in accordance I am persuaded with the unanimous sentiment of the whole House, that we shall feel we have lost one of our brightest ornaments, and whatever may be the honest variance of opinion on political questions, I know we must all be of one mind in regretting the absence of one as distinguished for every moral virtue as for the brilliancy of his talents.

"That retirement into more private life may

[1] Charles Manners Sutton, Speaker of the House of Commons, 1817-1834; created Viscount Canterbury 1835; died 1845.

contribute largely to your personal ease, and to the entire restoration of your health, is, my dear sir, the sincere wish of your most faithful and respectful

"Friend and servant,

"C. MANNERS SUTTON."

Lord John Russell's answer to Wilberforce's anti-bribery suggestions at the time of the first Reform Bill is given below. It is marked "kind and pleasing" by Wilberforce.

Lord John Russell to Mr. Wilberforce.

"SOUTH AUDLEY STREET,

"*June* 3.

"MY DEAR SIR,—I was very much gratified at receiving your letter, not only for the kind sentiments personally expressed towards me, but still more for the high testimony of your authority in favour of the course I have been pursuing. The resolutions I lately moved were directed against the very practice of which you complain in your letter; only instead of an election committee I propose a separate public committee for the purpose. The expenses of an election committee are such as to deter any from seeking that remedy but a candidate who has hopes of acquiring the seat himself, and the public is wronged for want of some one bound over to prosecute these offences.

After all, we must trust more to the frequent

canvassing of the question, and the improvement of moral feeling, which may be expected from education, than to the letter of any law that we can frame.

"I showed your letter to Mr. Pitt and Mr. Wynne, and should have been glad to have read it to the House, but I did not like to do so without your permission. Wishing you many years of happiness in your retirement, enhanced by reflecting on the usefulness of your past life,

"I remain, yours faithfully,

"J. RUSSELL."

Wilberforce writes on the same subject in October, 1831, to an old friend:—

"I cannot but think the Lords managed it very ill not to attempt the discovery of some compromise, giving up the rotten boroughs, granting members to great towns, accepting the new county members, and yet somewhat raising the qualification (surely no pauper should have the right of voting); this must at least have prevented the common fraud now practised on the people, that of imputing to those who voted at all against the Bill that they wished to retain all the worst abuses, which, in fact, they were as willing as the reformers to abolish. But I must break off. You, and I hope I, are prompted to say with old Hooker, I have lived long enough to see that the world is made up of perturbations. But, blessed be God, there remaineth a rest for the people of God. May I be permitted to meet you there, my dear sir."

On the different effects of the Oxford and Cambridge system on the minds of young men, Wilberforce writes to a friend:—

Mr. Wilberforce to Mr. William Gray.

"*December* 31, 1830.

"It is curious to observe the effects of the Oxford system in producing on the minds of young men a strong propensity to what may be termed Tory principles. From myself and the general tenour of our family and social circle, it might have been supposed that my children, though averse to party, would be inclined to adopt Liberal or, so far as would be consistent with party, Whig principles, but all my three Oxonians are strong friends to High Church and King doctrines. The effects I myself have witnessed would certainly induce me, had I to decide on the University to which any young protegé of mine should go, were he by natural temper or any other causes too prone to excess on the Tory side, I should decidedly send him to Cambridge, Trinity; were the opposite the case he should be fixed at Oriel, Oxford.

"As for the gentleman you mention,[1] his character is not to be expressed in a few words. Of his extraordinary powers no one ever entertained a doubt. There are also very pleasing traits of private character: I have been assured of his incessant and kind attentions to his old mother. On his brother's failing, I believe, in business, he paid his debts to a large amount and took on himself, I am assured, before being in office, the charge of his eight or nine children. Of his own little girl he was excessively fond, and he was always kind in what concerned friends or acquaintances. I cannot also but hope that he has seen so much of religious men as almost to have superior confidence in them. But you suppose me to be more personally acquainted with him than I am."

The next letter, to Mr. Manning, contains an allusion to his son Henry, afterwards Cardinal Manning, of whom it will be noted that Wilberforce "forms sanguine hopes that he will be a blessing to his fellow creatures."

At the time the letter was written, Wilberforce's large fortune had been seriously diminished, though he was far from being, as his letter would lead one to suppose, in the same unfortunate position as Mr. Manning.[2] The effect of his own loss was

---

[1] Mr., afterwards Lord, Brougham.
[2] Mr. Manning became bankrupt in the winter of 1830-31.

as he says, "greatly to augment his happiness." Enough was left for his comfort. It is true he gave up his home, and was no longer able to practise indiscriminate hospitality; also his subscriptions had to be curtailed, such as those to the York charities, as to which he "had been reminded in 1831 that they were larger than those of any other subscriber."

Mr. Wilberforce to Mr. Manning.

"*June* 11, 1832.

"I am truly rejoiced, my dear friend, to hear that you are so comfortably circumstanced. I also have abundant cause for thankfulness. The loss of fortune was graciously delayed in my instance until all my children having been educated, and two of them supplied with comfortable residences (Robert, my second son, recently by the perfectly spontaneous kindness of Lord Brougham), so that the effect of my loss of fortune has been greatly to augment Mrs. W.'s and my own happiness. What can be more delightful than to be the daily witness of our children having a large measure of conjugal happiness, the best of this world's goods, while at the same time they are discharging conscientiously and zealously the important duties of the pastoral office. It gave me real pleasure that your son had given up the situation at the Treasury for the Church. I have heard such an account of him from my sons, as gives me reason to form sanguine hopes that he will be a blessing to his fellow creatures."

The next extract refers to the painting of the well-known picture of Wilberforce now in the National Portrait Gallery.

Sir Thomas Lawrence to Mr. Wilberforce.

"You make a too flattering apology for sending me but your name in your own handwriting. I hardly know what other word in our language could boast of equal interest, and you may be assured, my dear sir, that by those the nearest to me it will be equally prized when the person to whom it is written can no longer produce it as evidence of his too fortunate career."

The date of the following lines of Cowper and also of Hayley is not given. They are marked "Verses sent to me by Cowper and Hayley."

To William Wilberforce, Esqre.

SONNET.

Thy country, Wilberforce, with just disdain,
    Hears thee by cruel men and impious called
    Fanatic, for thy zeal to loose th' enthralled
From exile, public sale, and slav'ry's chain.
    Friend of the poor, the wronged, the fetter gall'd,
Fear not lest labour such as thine be vain.
    Thou hast achieved a part—hast gained the ear
Of Britain's senate to thy glorious cause;

Hope smiles, joy springs, and though cold caution pause
   And weave delay, the better hour is near
   That shall remunerate thy toils severe
By peace for Afric fenced with British laws.
    Enjoy what thou hast won, esteem and love
    From all the good on earth, and all the Blest above!
                             WILLIAM COWPER.

To William Wilberforce, Esqre, on the preceding Sonnet.

When Virtue saw with brave disdain
Lucre's infuriate sons profane
   Her Wilberforce's worth;
As she beheld with generous ire,
His image fashioned for the fire
   Of diabolic mirth:

"Firm friend of suffering slaves!" she cried,
"These frantic outrages deride,
   While I protect thy name!
Soon shall one dear selected hand
Richly o'erpay at my command,
   Indignity with Fame:

"Since thou hast won, in Nature's cause,
My fondest love, my prime applause,
   Thy Honour is my care;
Now shall my favourite Bard be thine:
My Cowper, guard of glory's shine!
   Shall grave thy merits there."
                             WILLIAM HAYLEY.

BIRTHPLACE OF WILLIAM WILBERFORCE, AT HULL.

HOME LETTERS

HOME LETTERS.

The family letters which follow are some of a religious character, while others turn on more general topics.

Four letters written by Wilberforce to his daughter Elizabeth, aged fifteen at the date the correspondence begins, show the care with which he instilled into her mind all that he considered of most moment; also how he exercised "the privilege of a friend," for such he considered himself to his daughter, and "told her frankly all her faults."

Mr. Wilberforce to his daughter Elizabeth.

"*November* 30, 1816.

"This is but a short letter to my dear Elizabeth. When I do address my dear girl, I ought to consider how I can best testify my friendship: for friendship let there be between us; never can you have a friend more warmly attached to you or more interested in your welldoing and happiness than myself. But if we are to be friends, you must allow me the privilege of a friend, a privilege by far the most valuable of all its excellencies. So thought your dear Uncle Stephen,[1] when in the very extreme bitterness of his grief, which was as great as that of any one I ever witnessed, though he is now able to control his feelings before company, he said to me while enlarging on the various particulars of my dear sister's extraordinary character, 'O, she was a friend to my soul! She told me frankly all my faults,' an office in which, I am obliged to confess, he charged me with having been deficient. This has arisen, however, solely from my scarcely ever having seen him alone, when only I could converse with him confidentially. But if I am to exercise this best prerogative, this most sacred and indispensable duty of friendship, it will be necessary for my dear Elizabeth to prepare her mind and temper for receiving it properly, and for deriving from it all the benefits it is capable of imparting. Shall I be honest, and I must be so or be silent; were I otherwise, the very sheet which I am writing would rise up in judgment against me at the last day; if then, I am frank and honest, I must declare to you, that it is on this quarter that it will be necessary for my dear girl to guard herself with the utmost watchfulness, and, still more, to *prepare herself* with conscientious

[1] Mr. James Stephen married Wilberforce's sister.

care. This is what St. Paul terms "exercising herself to maintain a conscience void of offence towards God and towards man": what the Book of Proverbs styles, "keeping the heart *with all diligence:*" for unless we have accustomed ourselves to *self-suspicion*, if I may use such a phrase, we never benefit as we might from the friendly reproofs of a real friend. We may receive his remarks with civility, and even give him credit for his kind intentions, but we shall be almost sure to let it appear to any acute observer at least, that we rather tolerate his frankness out of principle, or put up with it in consideration of the friendly motives by which it has been prompted, than that we listen to it with a sincere desire of profiting from it, still less that we welcome it as one of the most valuable services in design, even when not in fact, that could be rendered to us. The grand preparation that is needed is, Humility; that sense of our own infirmities and our own weakness, which is felt by every true, at least by every flourishing Christian. We read in the Scripture that 'our hearts are deceitful above all things:' by which is meant, that we are all prone to flatter ourselves, to form too high an estimate of our own good qualities, and too low an idea of our bad ones. Now it is the first office of the Holy Spirit to teach us to know ourselves, and immediately to *suspect* ourselves as the first effect of that knowledge. Now be honest with yourself, my very dear child. Have you been accustomed to distrust the judgment you have been in the habit of forming of your own character, as you would have done if it had been formed and stated to you by any one whom you knew to be a notorious liar? Yet this is really the way in which we ought to feel; I know how difficult it is in practice from my own experience; and because it is so difficult, it is here that we need the special aid of the Holy Spirit, and should earnestly pray for His blessed influence to teach us to know ourselves. Be earnest, then, in prayer, my very dear Elizabeth, and frequent in self-examination on this very point. I have often detected my own self-partiality and self-deceit by observing how differently the same fault, be it small or great, appears to me when committed by myself, and when committed by others, how much more ready I am with apologies for it, or with extenuations for its guilt. If a servant has done anything wrong, or omitted some act of duty, I observe *how* it appears to me, and if I have done much the same fault, or been guilty of the same omission, how much less does it impress itself on me, how much sooner do I forget it. I assure you, I speak sincerely when I tell you I find this the case with myself: now observe whether you do; and if so, then it will be a subject for humiliation before God, and a motive for earnest prayer. Let my dearest Lizzie be particularly watchful to improve the present season; for as you have heard me say, Christ—as is stated in Rev. iii.—'stands at the door and knocks,' that is, He uses particular events and circumstances of our lives, for impressing us with the importance of spiritual things, and if the event and the circumstances pass over without producing their proper effect, there is always a positive bad consequence. So much grace is, as it were expended on us in vain. The heart becomes harder and less favourably disposed on another occasion. And though we must not limit the grace and power of God, yet it is a great point to know what the Scripture (2 Cor. vi.) terms "our appointed time, our day of salvation." I am sure you find your heart softened and affected more than usual just now. O try, my beloved girl, to render this permanently, let me say eternally, useful to you. I understand you are reading Doddridge's 'Rise and Progress.' You cannot read a better book. I hope it was one of the means of turning my heart to God. Certainly, there are few books which have been so extensively useful. Pray over some of the prayers at the conclusion of the chapters; as, for instance, if I remember right, that at the end of the chapter, 'After a state of spiritual decay.' But I have not the book at hand, and cannot quote it from memory. Don't read this till you have half an hour's leisure."

Of the privilege of friendship alluded to in this letter, Wilberforce also writes later to his daughter Elizabeth: "You will never find telling Robert" (afterwards Archdeacon Wilberforce), "of any fault offend him, if you do it when you are *tête à tête*, and when he sees from your manner and from the circumstances that you can only have his happiness at heart, I mean that this friendly regard can alone prompt you to such a proof of real attachment."

Mr. Wilberforce to his daughter Elizabeth.

"HASTINGS,

"*January* 17, 1817.

"MY DEAREST LIZZY,—Your letter to-day gives me pleasure. We heard from Marianne (Thornton) of her having paid you a visit. Her friendly attachment to Barbara[1] and you, I account as one of the special blessings of Providence; and there are many particulars, though not all, in which I should be very glad to have her the object of your imitation. I am half asleep from not having had a good night, and find myself occasionally writing one word in-

[1] Mr. Wilberforce's second daughter.

stead of another—a slip which I sometimes witness in my dear Lizzy's case; I know not whether it be from the same cause, I hope not. For my last night's wakefulness arose in part from my thinking on some subjects of deep interest from which, though I made several efforts, I could not altogether withdraw my thoughts. My mind obeyed me indeed while I continued wide awake, but when dropping half asleep, it started aside from the serious and composing train of ideas to which I had forced it up, and like a swerving horse, it chose to go its own way rather than mine. It is a delightful consideration, my dearest child, that there is a gracious and tender Saviour who, in our sleeping as well as waking hours, is watching over us for good, if we are of the number of those who look to Him habitually for consolation and peace, and such I trust will be more and more the case of my dear Elizabeth."

The next letter is in a more lively strain and explains to Elizabeth the system of Bishop Berkeley.

Mr. Wilberforce to his daughter Elizabeth.

"HIGHWOOD HILL,
"*July* 13, 1830.

"MY DEAR LIZZY,—If many intentions to write could be admitted as making up one letter, you would have to thank me for being so good a correspondent. But I fear that this is a mode of calculation that will only come into use, when the system of good Bishop Berkeley has become established. I cannot explain what this is so well as Robert could, but its distinctive principle is that there are no such things as substances. You may suppose that you have had the pleasure of re-visiting a very dear friend, called Miss Palmer, and you probably would assure me, if I asked you whether they still continued at the Hall any such vulgar practice as that of eating, that the turkies and fowls were as good and as freely bestowed as when I used to partake of them in earlier years. All mere delusion. All imagination. All ideal. There is no Elizabeth (she only *appeared* to occupy an ideal place in an ideal carriage, when she travelled down to Mosely and Elmdon), there is no Miss Palmer, nor are the fowls and turkies a whit more substantial than the supposed eaters of them. I really am serious— such is the system of one of the ablest and best of men (he was spoken of by Pope as 'Having every virtue under heaven'); he held that the Almighty formed us so as to have impressions produced on us, as if these were realities, but that this was all. I little intended when I took up my pen to give you such a Lecture in Metaphysics. I am sure I have had a Lecture, a practical one, on the duty of bearing interruptions with good humour. This morning (it is now 4 p.m. and dinner taking on the table) I took up my pen at 10 o'clock, and my first thoughts were naturally drawn to you. Scarcely had I finished my first sentence when in came Knowles (as queer he is as ever) and announced Lord Teignmouth. Up I went to him in the drawing-room, and as cordial a shake of the hand he received from me as one friend can give to another. But I own I began to wish I could be in two places at once. I had secured as I thought, several hours of quiet, and my eyes happened to be better than for sometime past, and I was therefore hoping to pay away a great part of my epistolary arrears, when in comes my friend, and remains with me between three and four hours, refusing to stay dinner, but not departing till after the post had gone out. However, such incidents are salutary, they accustom us to bear with cheerfulness the little vexatious interruptions which people sometimes bear with less equanimity than more serious grievances. Here enter Uncle Stephen——But with some pressing I have got him to agree to stay till to-morrow morning, so I may finish my letter. I must first tell you what I think a remarkably well-expressed description of Lady Raffles, contained in a letter from the Duchesse de Broglie, to whom I gave Lady R. a letter of introduction—'C'est une personne qui inspire un profond interêt. Elle a tant de dignité et de douceur.' The epithets appear to me very happy. And now, my dear Lizzy, I must conclude my very disjointed letter, written *à plusiers reprises* as the French phrase it."

Elizabeth would seem to have written to her father as to her solitariness of spirit in so confidential a strain that his sympathy had been thoroughly awakened. In his answer he excuses himself for not having been more of a companion to her on the ground that he had been so long engaged in public business, and also that as he had been almost an old bachelor before he married, he had got out of the habit of tender attention to young women of education and delicacy; but he assures her she will always find in him unfeigned tenderness of spirit for all her feelings, and all her infirmities. His remedies for "solitariness of spirit" are most practical.

Mr. Wilberforce to his daughter Elizabeth.
"HIGHWOOD HILL,
"*July* 26, 1830.

"MY VERY DEAR LIZZY,—Though, owing to my having been betrayed into forgetfulness of the flight of time while sitting under the shade of the lime tree it is now so late that I shall not be able to write to you so fully as I wished and intended, I must not be so unjust to myself or so unkind to you as I certainly should be if I were not to reply to your last interesting letter as soon as possible. And yet, my dear girl, it could be only from nervous sensibility that you could doubt of my putting the right construction on your opening your heart to me without disguise. I wish you could have seen the whole interior of mine when I had read through it: I am not ashamed to say that I melted into tears of affectionate sympathy. Your letter really contained nothing but what tended to call forth feelings of esteem and regard for you. My dear Lizzy, I will return your openness by a similar display of it. I will confess to you that I have not seldom blamed myself for not endeavouring more to cheer your solitary hours, when you have had no friend of your own sex to whom you could open your heart, and I will try to amend of this fault. My not walking with you more frequently has, however, been often caused by the circumstance you mention, that at the very hour at which I can get out, just when the post has departed, you are yourself employed in a way of which I always think with pleasure, and which I doubt not will bring down a blessing on your head. But there is another cause which may have some effect in rendering me less tenderly attentive than young women of education and delicacy like persons to be, and must in some measure find them, before they can open their hearts to them with unreserved freedom. I allude to my having been so long and so constantly engaged in public business and having been almost an old bachelor before I married. Let my dear child, however, be assured that she will always experience from me an unfeigned tenderness of spirit and a kind consideration for all her feelings and even, shall I say it, all her infirmities. Meanwhile let me advise you, my dear child, whenever you do feel anything of that solitariness of spirit of which you speak, to endeavour to find an antidote for it in prayer. There is often much of bodily nervousness in it. I am ashamed to acknowledge that I am sometimes conscious of it myself. Another method which I would recommend to you for getting the better of it, is to engage in some active exertion, teaching some child, instructing some servant, comforting some poor sufferer from poverty and sickness. I deeply feel the Bishop and Mrs. Ryder's kindness to you, but it is of a piece with all their conduct towards me and mine. God bless them, I say from the heart."

In 1814, Mr. Wilberforce at the age of fifty-five, begins his correspondence with his son Samuel, aged nine. The father is already seeking for a proof of the grand change of conversion in his child.

Mr. Wilberforce to his son Samuel.
"*September* 13, 1814.

"I was shocked to hear that you are nine years

old; I thought it was eight. You must take great pains to prove to me that you are nine not in years only, but in head and heart and mind. Above all, my dearest Samuel, I am anxious to see decisive marks of your having begun to undergo the *great change.* I come again and again to look to see if it really be begun, just as a gardener walks up again and again to examine his fruit trees and see if his peaches are set; if they are swelling and becoming larger, finally if they are becoming ripe and rosy. I would willingly walk barefoot from this place to Sandgate to see a clear proof of the *grand change* being begun in my dear Samuel at the end of my journey."[1]

"*March* 25, 1817.

"I do hope, my dear Samuel, like his great namesake at a still earlier period of life, is beginning to turn in earnest to his God. Oh, remember prayer is the great means of spiritual improvement, and guard as you would against a wild beast which was lying in a bush by which you were to pass, ready to spring upon you—guard in like manner, I say, against wandering thoughts when you are at prayer either by yourself or in the family.[2] Nothing

[1] Part of this letter is in "Life of Wilberforce."

[2] This thought, thus strongly impressed on Samuel's mind, was many years afterwards expanded by him into the lovely allegory of the "Children and the Lion," published in "Agathos and other Stories."

grieves the Spirit more than our willingly suffering our thoughts to wander and fix themselves on any object which happens at the time to interest us."

"*June* 5, 1817.

"MY DEAR SAMUEL,—Loving you as dearly as I do, it might seem strange to some thoughtless people that I am glad to hear you are unhappy. But as it is about your soul, and as I know that a short unhappiness of this kind often leads to lasting happiness and peace and joy, I cannot but rejoice. I trust, my dear boy, it is the Spirit of God knocking at the door of your heart, as the Scripture expresses it, and making you feel uneasy, that you may be driven to find pardon and the sanctifying influences of the Holy Spirit, and so be made one of Christ's flock and be taken care of in this world and be delivered from hell, and be taken when you die, whether sooner or later, to everlasting happiness in heaven. My dearest boy, whenever you feel in this way, I beseech you, get alone and fall on your knees, and pray as earnestly as you can to God for Christ's sake to forgive you and to sanctify you, and in short to make you to be born again, as our Saviour expressed it to Nicodemus."

"*July* 19*th*.

"I will procure and send you Goldsmith's 'Grecian History,' if you will read it attentively, though it is by no means so good a history as Mitford's; it is little better than an epitome. Let me tell you I was pleased with your skeleton of Mr. Langston's sermon, and I should be glad of such another bag of bones. My dear boy, whenever you feel any meltings of mind, any sorrow for sin, or any concern about your soul, do not, I beg of you, stifle it or turn away your thoughts to another subject, but get alone and pray to God to hear and bless you, to take away the stony heart and substitute a heart of flesh in its place."

"*August* 15*th*, 1817.

"The great rule practically for pleasing our Saviour in all the little events of the day is to be thinking of Him occasionally and trying to please Him, by not merely not doing evil, but by doing good; not merely negatively trying not to be unkind, not to be disobedient, not to give pain, but trying positively, to *be kind*, to be obedient, to give pleasure."

"*November* 1, 1817.

"MY VERY DEAR SAMUEL,—Though some company who are to dine with me are already in the drawing-room, I must leave them to themselves for two minutes while I express the very great pleasure I have received from Mr. Marsh's account of both my dear boys. Being a political economist, I cannot but admit the beneficial effects which always flow from the division of labour, and must therefore rather commend than blame the instance of it which is afforded by your writing the letter while Bob is building the house. It is quite a drop of balm into my heart when I hear of my dear boys going on well."

"*May* 2, 1818.

"Could you both but look into my heart and there see the tender and warm love I feel for you! How my heart bleeds at the idea of your being drawn into the paths of sin and bringing the grey hairs of your poor old father with sorrow to the grave—a most unlikely issue I do really hope; and, on the other hand, could you witness the glow of affection which is kindled by the prospect of your becoming the consolation of my declining years, you would want no more powerful motives to Christian obedience."

"*April* 25, 1818.

"Our West Indian warfare is begun, and our opponents are commencing in the way of some (I won't add an epithet) classes of enemies by the poisoned arrows of calumny and falsehood. But how thankful should we be to live in a country in which the law protects us from personal injury!"

"*June* 26, 1818.

"My dear children little think how often we parents are ruminating about them when we are absent from them, perhaps in very bustling scenes like that from which I come. Mr. Babington is a candidate for the county of Leicester, and I really trust he will succeed; the two other candidates are Lord Robert Manners, the Duke of Rutland's brother, and Mr. Phillips, a country gentleman of large property. My dear Samuel, keep going on well. Prayer and self-denial, as you used to be taught when a very little boy, are the grand things."

"*February* 13, 1819.

"I am very glad that you like your new situation. One of the grand secrets to be remembered, in order to enable us to pass through life with comfort, is not to expect too much from any new place or plan, or from the accomplishment of any new purpose."

"*March* 12, 1819.

"On the whole, Mr. Hodson's report of you is a gratifying one. But there is one ground for doubts and fears, and I hope my beloved child will endeavour to brighten that quarter of my prospect. I fear you do not apply to your business with energy. This, remember, was your fault at Mr. Marsh's, and you alleged, not without plausibility, that this arose in a great degree from your wanting spirits, in consequence of your having no playfellows for your hours of recreation, no schoolmates for your season of business. A horse never goes so cheerfully alone as when animated by the presence of a companion, and a boy profits from the same quickening principle. But my dearest Samuel has not now this danger to plead at Mr. Hodson's, and I hope he will now bear in mind that this indisposition to work strenuously [1] is one of his besetting sins." [2]

"*May* 22, 1819.

"I hear with pleasure of your goings on, and I may add that we all thought our dear boy greatly improved when he was last with us. How delightful will it be to me in my declining years to hear that my dearest Samuel is doing credit to his name and family!"

"*May* 25, 1819.

"I do not like to write merely on the *outside* of this cover, though I have time to insert very little within, yet as when you were a little boy I used to delight in taking a passing kiss of you, so now it is quite gratifying to exchange a salutation with you on paper, though but for a minute or two. The sight of my handwriting will call forth in the mind of my dear, affectionate Samuel all those images of parental and family tenderness with

---

[1] Bishop Wilberforce once told Dr. Woodford (Bishop of Ely) that he was naturally indolent and had at first "to flog himself up to his work" (Life, vol. iii. p. 305). To those who remember Bishop Wilberforce, and to readers of his Life, these passages must appear surprising indeed. They afford a striking instance of a natural defect turned into the contrary Christian grace.

[2] Part of this letter is in the "Life of Wilberforce."

which the Almighty permits us to be refreshed when children or parents are separated from each other far asunder. You have a Heavenly Father, too, my dearest boy, who loves you dearly, and who has promised He will never leave you nor forsake you if you will but devote yourself to His service in His appointed way. And so I trust you are resolved to do. I hope you got your parcel safe, and that the lavender-water had not oozed out of the bottle; the cork did not seem tight. Farewell, my very dear Samuel."

"*September* 17, 1819.

"My dear Boy,—It is a great pleasure to me that you wish to know your faults. Even if we are a little nettled when we first hear of them, especially when they are such as we thought we were free from, or such as we are ashamed that others should discover, yet if we soon recover our good-humour, and treat with kindness the person who has told us of them, it is a very good sign. It may help us to do this to reflect that such persons are rendering us, even when they themselves may not mean it, but may even only be gratifying their own dislike of us, the greatest almost of all services, perhaps may be helping us to obtain an eternal increase of our happiness and glory. For we never should forget that though we are reconciled to God through the atoning blood of Christ, altogether freely and of mere undeserved mercy, yet when once reconciled, and become the children of God, the degrees of happiness and glory which He will grant to us will be proportioned to the degree of holiness we have obtained, the degree (in other words) in which we have improved the talents committed to our stewardship."

"WEYMOUTH, *September*, 1820.

"I have this day learned for the first time that there were to be oratorios at Gloucester, and that some of the boys were to go to them. I will be very honest with you. When I heard that the cost was to be half a guinea, I greatly doubted whether it would be warrantable to pay such a sum for such a performance for such *youth*. This last consideration has considerable weight with me, both as it renders the pleasure of the entertainment less, and as at your early age the sources of pleasure are so numerous. But my difficulties were all removed by finding that the money would not merely be applied to the use of tweedledum and tweedledee (though I write this, no one is fonder than myself of music), but was to go to the relief of the clergy widows and children. I say therefore yes. Q.E.D."

"*September* 4, 1820.

"I am persuaded that my dear Samuel will

endeavour to keep his mind in such a right frame as to enable him to enjoy the pleasures of the scenes through which he is passing, and to be cheered by the consciousness that he is now carrying forward all the necessary agricultural processes in order to his hereafter reaping a rich and abundant harvest. Use yourself, dear boy, to take time occasionally for reflection. Let this be done especially before you engage in prayer, a duty which I hope you always endeavour to perform with all possible seriousness. As I have often told you, it is the grand test by which the state of a Christian may always be best estimated."

"BATH, *September* 23, 1820.

"Did you ever cross a river with a horse in a ferry boat? If so, you must have observed, if you are an observing creature, which if you are not I beg you will become with all possible celerity, that the said horse is perfectly quiet after he is once fairly in the boat—a line of conduct in which it would be well if this four-footed navigator were imitated by some young bipeds I have known in their aquatic exercitations. And so said animal continues—the quadruped I mean, mind—perfectly quiet until he begins to approach the opposite shore. Then he begins to show manifest signs of impatience by dancing and frisking sometimes to such a degree as to overset the boat, to the no small injury of others (for whom he very little cares) as well as himself. This is what may be well called making more haste than good speed. None the less, though I am fully aware that the same frisking quadruped is a very improper subject of imitation, not only to an old biped but to an experienced M.P. of forty years' standing, yet I find myself in a state of mind exactly like that of the horse above mentioned, though it has not the same effects on my animal powers, and though, being on dry land and in a parlour, not a boat, I might frisk away if I chose with perfect impunity to myself and others. But to quit metaphor which I have fairly worn out, or, rather, rode to death, when I was a hundred miles from my dear Samuel, though my affection for him was as strong and my sentiments and feelings as much employed in him as now, yet these are now accompanied with an impatient longing to extinguish the comparatively little distance that is between us, and to have my dearest boy not only in my heart but in my arms, and yet on reflection this very feeling is beneficial. I recollect that our separation is an act of self-denial, and I offer it up to my Saviour with a humble sense of His goodness, in subjecting me to such few and those comparatively such easy crosses. My dearest Samuel will remember to have our blessed Lord continually in remembrance, and by associating Him thus with all the little circumstances of life, it is that we are to live in His love and fear continually."

"*November* 20, 1820.

"We quite enjoyed your pleasure in Robert's visit. In truth the gratification we parents derive from our children's innocent, much more their commendable, enjoyments is one of the greatest of our pleasures."

"BATH, *November* 18, 1820.

"MY DEAR SAMUEL.—I am sorry to hear that your examination is, or part of it at least, disadvantageous to you. Does not this arise in part from your having stayed with us when your schoolfellows were at Maisemore? If so, the lesson is one which, if my dear boy duly digests it and bottles it up for future use, may be a most valuable one for the rest of his life. It illustrates a remark which I well remember in Bishop Butler's 'Analogy,' that our faults often bring on some bad consequence long after they have been committed, and when they perhaps have been entirely banished from our memory. Some self-indulgence perhaps may have lost us an advantage, the benefit of which might have extended through life. But it is due to my dear Samuel to remark that, though his stay was protracted a very little out of self-indulgence (as much ours as his), yet it was chiefly occasioned by the necessity of his going up to London on account of his ancle. (By the way, tell me in two words—ancle better or worse or *idem*.) But my Samuel must not vex himself with the idea of falling below the boy who has commonly been his competitor, owing to his stay having prevented his reading what is to be in part the subject of the examination. It would really be quite wrong to feel much on this account, and that for several reasons. First, everybody about you will know the disadvantages under which you start, and will make allowances accordingly. Next, if you do as well or better in the parts you *have* read, you will show the probability of your having done well in the other also, if you had possessed with it the same advantage. And what I wish my dearest boy seriously to consider is, that any uneasiness he might feel on account of this circumstance would deserve no better a name than emulation, which the apostle enumerates as one of the lusts of the flesh. You should do your business and try to excel in it, to please your Saviour, as a small return for all He has done for you, but a return which He will by no means despise. It is this which constitutes the character of a real Christian : that, considering himself as bought with a price—viz., that of the blood of Jesus Christ—he regards it as his duty to try and please his Saviour in everything. And to be honest with you, my very dear boy, let me tell you that it appears to me very probable that the Heavenly Shepherd, whose tender care of His people is, you must remember, described to us as like that of a shepherd towards the tender lambs of his flock, may have designed by this very incident to discover to you that you were too much under the influence of emulation, and to impress you with a sense of the duty of rooting it out. Emulation has a great tendency to lessen love. It is scarcely possible to have a fellow-feeling (that is, duly to sympathise) with any one if we are thinking much about, and setting our hearts on, getting before him, or his not getting before us. This disposition of mind, which includes in it an over-estimation of the praise of our fellow-creatures, is perhaps the most subtle and powerful of all our corruptions, and that which costs a real Christian the most trouble and pain; for he will never be satisfied in his mind unless the chief motive in his mind and feelings is the way to please his Saviour. The best way to promote the right temper of mind will be after earnest prayer to God to bless your endeavours, to try to keep the idea of Jesus Christ and of His sufferings, and of the love which prompted Him willingly to undergo them, in your mind continually, and especially when you are going to do, occasionally when you are doing, your business. And then recollect that He has declared He will kindly accept as a tribute of gratitude whatever we do to please Him, and call to mind all His kindness, all His sacrifices; what glory and happiness He left, what humiliation and shame and agony He endured; and then reflect that the only return He, who is then, remember, at that very moment actually looking upon you, expects from you, is that you should remember His Heavenly Father who sent Him, and Him Himself, and (as I said before) endeavour to please Him. This He tells us is to be done by keeping God's commandments. And my dear Samuel knows that this obedience must be universal—all God's commandments. Not that we shall be able actually to do this; but then we must wish and desire to do it. And when, from our natural corruption, infirmities do break out we must sincerely lament them, and try to guard against them in future. Thus a true Christian endeavours to have the idea of his Saviour continually present with him. To do his business as the Scripture phrases it, unto the Lord and not unto men. To enjoy his gratifications as allowed to him by his merciful and kind Saviour, who knows that we need recreations, and when they are neither wrong in kind nor excessive in degree they may and should be enjoyed with a grateful recollection of Him who intends for us still nobler and higher pleasures hereafter. This is the very perfection of religion; 'Whether we eat or drink or whatever we do, do all to the glory of God.'

"All I am now contending for is that my dearest Samuel may at least endeavour to do his school business with a recollection of his Saviour, and a wish to please Him, and when he finds the feeling of emulation taking the place of this right principle look up and beg God's pardon for it, and implore the Holy Spirit's help to enable you to feel as you ought and wish to feel. But let me also ask my dear Samuel to reflect if he did not stay too long at home in the last holidays. Too much prosperity and self-indulgence (and staying at home may be said to be a young person's indulgence and prosperity) are good neither for man nor boy, neither for you nor for myself."[1]

"DOWNING STREET, *December* 11, 1820.

"Three words, or, rather, five lines, just to assure you that in the midst of all our Parliamentary business I do not forget my very dear Samuel; on the contrary, he is endeared to me by all the turbulence of the element in which I commonly breathe, as I thereby am led still more highly to prize and, I hope, to be thankful to God for

[1] Part of this letter is in Bishop Wilberforce's Life.

domestic peace and love. Pray God bless you, my dearest boy, and enable you to devote to Him your various faculties and powers."

The mutual affection of father and son is touchingly shown in many passages scattered through their letters. Two may serve as specimens:—

"*February* 24, 1821.

"Perhaps at the very time of your being occupied in reading my sentiments, I may be engaged in calling you up before my mind's eye and recommending you to the throne of grace."

"*September* 5.

"Probably at the very same time you will be thinking of me and holding a conversation with me."

"LONDON, *June* 30, 1821.

"MY VERY DEAR BOY,—I congratulate you cordially on your success, and I rejoice to hear of your literary progress. But I should have been still more gratified, indeed beyond all comparison more, had Mr. Hodson's certificate of your scholarship been accompanied, as it formerly was, with an assurance that you were advancing in the still more important particulars of self-control, of humility, of love—in short, in all the various forms and phases, if I may so term them, which St. Paul ascribes to it in his beautiful eulogium (1 Cor. xiii.). Oh, my dear boy, I should be even an unnatural father instead of what I trust I am, an affectionate one, if, believing as I do, and bearing in mind that you are an immortal being who must be happy or miserable for ever, I were not, above all things, anxious to see you manifest those buds and shoots which alone are true indications of a celestial plant, the fruits of which are the produce of the Garden of God. My dear Samuel, be honest with yourself; you have enjoyed and still enjoy many advantages for which you are responsible. Use them *honestly;* that is, according to their just intention and fair employment and improvement. Above all things, my dearest boy, cultivate a spirit of prayer. Never hurry over your devotions, still less omit them. Farewell, my dearest boy."

"1821.

"In speaking of the pros and cons of Maisemore, you spoke of one great boy with whom you disagreed. I always meant to ask you about the nature, causes, and extent of your difference. And the very idea of a standing feud is so opposite to the Christian character that I can scarcely understand it. I can, however, conceive a youth of such crabbed and wayward temper that the only way of going on with him is that of avoiding all intercourse with him as much as possible. But, nine times out of ten, if one of two parties be really intent on healing the breach and preventing the renewal of it, the thing may be done. Now, my dear Samuel, may not you be partly in fault? If so, I beg of you to strive to get the better of it. I have recently had occasion to observe how much a frank and kind demeanour, when we conceive we have really just cause for complaint, disarms resentment and conciliates regard. Remember, my dearest boy, that you have enjoyed advantages which probably R. has not, and that therefore more Christian kindness and patience may be expected from you than from him. Again, you would be glad, I am sure, to produce in his mind an opinion favourable to true religion, and not that he should say, 'I don't see what effect Christianity has produced in Samuel Wilberforce.' Oh, my dear Samuel, I love you most affectionately, and I wish you could see how earnestly I long hereafter (perhaps from the world of spirits) to witness my dearest boy's progress into professional life that of a growing Christian, 'shining more and more into the perfect day.' My Samuel's conduct as it respects his studies, and, what I value much more, his disposition and behaviour, has been such for some time as to draw on him Mr. Hodson's eulogium, and so I trust he will continue doing."

"*October* 12, 1821.

"It is quite delightful to me to receive such an account of you as is contained in the letter Mama has this day had from Mr. Hodson. Oh that I may continue to have such reports of my dear Samuel wherever he may be. They quite warm his old father's heart, and melt his mother's."

"*February* 20, 1822.

"You never can have a friend, your dear affectionate mother alone excepted, whose interests and sympathies are so identically the same. Yet I have known instances in which, though children have been convinced in their understandings of this being the case between them and their parents, yet from not having begun at an early period of life to make a father a confidant, they could not bring themselves to do it when they grew older, but felt a strange shrinking back from opening their minds to the parent they cordially loved, and of whose love to them they were fully satisfied. I hope you will continue, my dear Samuel, to speak to me without constraint or concealment.

"The two chief questions you ask relate to Repentance and to Predestination. As to the former—sorrow for sin is certainly a part of it, but the degree of the feelings of different people will be as different as their various tempers and dispositions. If the same person whose feelings were very tender and susceptible on other topics and occasions were very cold in religion, that doubtless of itself is no good sign. But remember, repentance in the Greek means a change of heart, and the test of its sincerity is more its rendering us serious and watchful in our endeavours to abstain from sin and to practise known duty, than its causing many tears to flow, which effect may be produced in a susceptible nature with very little solid impression on the heart and character. The grand mark, I repeat it, of true repentance, is its providing a dread of sin and a watchfulness against it. As for Predestination, the subject is one the depths of which no human intellect can fathom. But even the most decided Predestinarians I have ever known have acknowledged that the invitations of God were made to all without exception, and that it was men's own fault that they did not accept these invitations. Again, does it not appear undeniably from one end of Scripture to the other that men's perishing, where they do perish, is always represented as their own bringing on? Indeed the passage in Ezekiel, 'As I live, saith the Lord, I have no pleasure in the death of a sinner, but that he should repent and live.' Again, do compare the ninth of Romans, in which that awful passage is contained: 'Hath not the potter power over the clay to make one vessel to honour, and another to dishonour? What if God,' &c., &c.; and compare this with Jeremiah, I think xviiith, to which passage St. Paul manifestly refers, and you will see there that the executing or remitting a threatening of vengeance is made to depend on the object of the threats turning from his evil way or continuing in it. This is very remarkable. Only pray, my dearest boy, and all will be well; and strive not to grieve the Holy Spirit. Before you actually engage in prayer always pause a minute or two and recollect yourself, and especially practise my rule of endeavouring to imagine myself in the presence of God, and to remember that to God all the bad actions, bad tempers, bad words of my whole life are all open in their entire freshness of circumstances and colouring; and when I recollect how I felt on the first committing of a wrong action, and then call to mind that to God sin must appear in itself far more hateful than to me, this reflection I often find to produce in me a deep humiliation; and then the promise is sure—the Lord is nigh to them that are of a contrite heart, and will save such as be of a humble spirit. I rejoice that it has pleased God to touch your heart. May I live, if it please God, to see you an honour to your family and a blessing to your fellow-creatures."

"*March* 30, 1822.

"It is scarcely possible for children to have an adequate conception of the delight it gives to a parent's heart to receive a favourable report of a dear child. And of late God has been very gracious to me in this particular. I trust I shall continue to enjoy such gratification, and that the day will come when my dear Samuel will in his turn become a parent and be solaced and cheered with such accounts as he himself will now furnish. And then, when I am dead and gone, he will remember his old father, and the letter he had from him on Sunday, 31st March, 1822."

"*April*, 1822.

"Though honestly my purse is in such a state that I cannot buy books except very sparingly, I beg you will buy Hume and Smollett, 13 vols. large 8vo, for £5 10s., and Gibbon's 'Rome' you may also purchase, if you wish it, for £4 10s., 12 vols. But you must take these two birthday presents for Scotch pints—each double. Had I as much money as I have good will you should wish for no book that I would not get you."

"*October* 22, 1822.

"The train of your idea and feelings is precisely that which I believe is commonly experienced at the outset of a religious course. It was my own, I am sure; I mean specially that painful apprehension of which you speak, lest your sorrow for sin should be less on account of its guilt than its danger, less on account of its hatefulness in the sight of God, and its ingratitude towards your Redeemer, than on that of its subjecting you to the wrath and punishment of God. But, my dear Samuel, blessed be God, we serve a gracious Master, a merciful Sovereign, who has denounced those threatenings for the very purpose of exciting our fears; and thereby being driven to flee from the wrath to come and lay hold on eternal life. By degrees the humble hope of your having obtained the pardon of your sins and the possession of the Divine favour will enable you to look up to God with feelings of filial confidence and love, and to Christ as to an advocate and a friend. The more you do this the better. Use yourself, my dearest Samuel, to take now and then a solitary walk, and in it to indulge in these spiritual meditations. The disposition to do this will gradually become a habit, and a habit of unspeakable value. I have long considered it as a great misfortune, or rather, I should say, as having been very injurious to your brother William, that he never courted solitude in his walks, or indeed at any time. Some people are too much inclined to it, I grant; they often thereby lose the inestimable benefit which results from having a friend to whom we open our hearts, one of the most valuable of all possessions both for this world and the next. When I was led into speaking of occasional intervals of solitude ('when Isaac, like the solitary saint, Walks forth to meditate at eventide,' you remember the passage, I doubt not), I was mentioning that holy, peaceful, childlike trust in the fatherly love of our God and Saviour which gradually diffuses itself through the soul and takes possession of it, when we are habitually striving to walk by faith under the influence of the Holy Spirit. When we allow ourselves to slacken or be indolent in our religious exercises, much more when we fall into actual sin, or have not watched over our tempers so as to be ashamed of looking our Heavenly Father in the face (if I may so express myself, I am sure with no irreverent meaning), then this holy confidence lessens and its diminution is a warning to us that we are going on ill. We must then renew our repentance and supplications, and endeavour to obtain a renewed supply of the blessed influences of the divine Spirit; and then we shall again enjoy the light of God's countenance. There are two or three beautiful sections in Doddridge's 'Rise and Progress' on these heads, and I earnestly recommend especially to you that, the subject of which is, I think, the Christian under the hiding of God's presence. I have been looking, and I find the section, or rather chapter I allude to, is that entitled, 'Case of spiritual decay and languor in religion.' There is a following one on 'Case of a relapse into known sin,' and I trust you have a pretty good edition of this super-excellent book.

"I have a word to say on another topic—that, I mean, of purity—the necessity of most scrupulous guarding against the very first commencement or even against the appearance of evil is in no instance so just and so important as in the case of all sins of this class. Many a man who would have been restrained from the commission of sins of this class by motives of worldly prudence or considerations of humanity, has been hurried into sin by not attending to this warning. I myself remember an instance of this kind in two people, both of whom I knew. And as Paley truly remarks that there is no class of vices which so depraves the character as illicit intercourse with the female sex, so he likewise mentions it as a striking proof of the superior excellence of Christ's moral precepts, that in the case of chastity and purity it lays the restraint on the *heart* and on the *thoughts* as the only way of providing against the grossest acts of disobedience. Oh, my dear Samuel, guard here with especial care, and may God protect and keep you. Indeed, I trust He will, and it is with exceeding pleasure that I think of you, and humbly and hopefully look forward on your advancing course in life. I did not intend saying half so much, but when I enter into conversation with my Samuel I know not how to stop. 'With thee conversing I forget all course of seasons and their change.'"

"*October* 26, 1822.

"I cannot to-day send you the account of *time*,

but I will transmit it to you. It was a very simple business, and the chief object was to take precautions against the disposition to waste time at breakfast and other *rendezvous*, which I have found in myself when with agreeable companions, and to prove to myself by the decisive test of figures that I was not working so hard as I should have supposed rom a general survey of my day. The grand point is to maintain an habitual sense of responsibility and to practise self-examination daily as to the past and the future day."

"*March* 17, 1822.

"No man has perhaps more cause for gratitude to God than myself. But of all the various instances of His goodness, the greatest of all, excepting only His Heavenly Grace, is the many kind friends with whom a Gracious Providence has blessed me. Oh remember, my dearest boy, to form friendships with those only who love and serve God, and when once you have formed them, then preserve them as the most valuable of all possessions.

"One of my chief motives now for paying visits is to cultivate the friendship of worthy people who, I trust, will be kind to my dearest children when I am no more. I hope you and the rest will never act so as to be unworthy of the connections I have formed."

"*November* 22, 1822.

"Robert Grant's[1] election has cost my eyes more than they could well expend on such a business. But both his hereditary, and his personal, claim to all I could do was irresistible. Your mother, Elizabeth, and I have of late been moving from place to place, staying a few days with the Whitmores, with the Gisbornes and Evans's, and from them with a Mr. Smith Wright and his wife, Lady Sitwell. She is a sensible, interesting woman. They live in a residence, Okeover, which is in the most beautiful part of Derbyshire, very near Dovedale, close to Ilam, &c. My dear Samuel will one day, I trust, delight himself in these beautiful and romantic vallies. My chief object in these visits was to provide future intimacies and I hope friendships for you and your brothers. And how thankful ought we to be, to be enabled thus to select for our associates the best families in so many different counties; best, I mean, in the true sense of the word, —men of real worth, who, I am sure, will always receive you with kindness for my sake. I often look up with gratitude to the Giver of all good,

---

[1] Born 1779, younger son of Wilberforce's intimate friend, Right Hon. Charles Grant. Robert was in Parliament, 1818-34: was Judge-Advocate-General: knighted, 1834, and made Governor-General of Bombay: a persistent advocate of Jewish emancipation: author of pamphlets on Indian affairs and many well-known hymns: died 1838.

for the favour with men—which it would be affectation not to confess where it is not improper to mention such things, that He has graciously given me, chiefly in the view of its ensuring for my children the friendly regard and personal kindnesses of many good people after I shall be laid low in the grave.

"I could have made them acquainted with great people, but I have always avoided it, from a conviction that such connections would tend neither to their temporal comfort in the long run, nor to the advancement of their eternal interests. But it is most gratifying to me to reflect that they will be known to some of the very best people in the kingdom, and to good people of other countries also. Oh, my dear Samuel, how thankful should we be to our Heavenly Father who has made our cup to overflow with mercies. How rich will our portion appear when compared with that of so many of our fellow-creatures. It used, when I was a bachelor especially, when I often spent my Sundays alone, to be my frequent Sunday habit to number up my blessings, and I assure you it is a most useful practice; *e.g.*, that I had been born in Great Britain, in such a century, such a part of it, such a rank in life, such a class and character of parents, then my personal privileges. But I have no time to-day for long conversation."

The next letter touches on topics of the day, and then refers to the son's question, Why had not his father a settled home? Evidently Samuel felt it a desolate arrangement, but Wilberforce, as was his wont, finds certain advantages in the very discomforts of the plan.

"*December* 5, 1822.

"I believe I never answered your question who it was that advised me to retire from Parliament. I entirely forget. Your question, Will there be war? I answer, I know no more than you do, but I am inclined to believe the French will attack Spain, very unadvisedly in my opinion, and I shall be surprised if the French Government itself, however priding itself on its policy, will not ultimately have reason to form the same judgment. . . . Never was there before a country on earth, the public affairs of which (for many years past at least I may affirm it,) were administered with such a simple and strong desire to promote the public welfare as those of Great Britain. And it is very remarkable that some of those very measures which were brought forward and carried through with the most general concurrence have subsequently appeared most doubtful. The present extreme distress of the agricultural class throughout the whole kingdom, is admitted by all to have been in some degree, by many to have been entirely, caused by our ill-managed if not ill-advised return to cash payments, in which nearly the whole of both Houses concurred. Surely this should teach us to be diffident in our judgments of others, and to hold our own opinions with moderation. In short, my dear Samuel, the best preparation for being a good politician, as well as a superior man in every other line, is to be a truly religious man. For this includes in it all those qualities which fit men to pass through life with benefit to others and with reputation to ourselves. Whatever is to be the effect produced by the subordinate machinery, the main-spring must be the desire to please God, which, in a Christian, implies faith in Christ and a grateful sense of the mercies of God through a Redeemer, and an aspiration after increasing holiness of heart and life. And I am reminded (you will soon see the connection of my ideas) of a passage in a former letter of yours about a home, and I do not deny that your remarks were very natural. Yet every human situation has its advantages as well as its evils. And if the want of a home deprive us of the many and great pleasures which arise out of the relations and associations, especially in the case of a large family, with which it is connected, yet there is an advantage, and of a very high order, in our not having this well-known anchoring ground, if I may so term it. We are less likely to lose the consciousness of our true condition in this life; less likely to forget that while sailing in the ocean of life we are always exposed to the buffeting of the billows, nay, more, to the rock and the quicksand. The very feeling of desolateness of which you speak—for I do not deny having formerly experienced some sensations of this kind, chiefly when I used to be long an inmate of the houses of friends who had wives and families to welcome them home again after a temporary absence—this very feeling led me, and taught me in some measure habitually to look upwards to my permanent and never failing inheritance, and to feel that I was to consider myself here as a pilgrim and a stranger who had no continuing city but who sought one to come. Yet this very conviction is by no means incompatible with the attachment and enjoyment of home-born pleasures, which doubtless are natural and virtuous pleasures, such as it gratifies me and fills me with hope to see that my very dear Sam relishes with such vivid delight, and that he looks forward to them with such grateful anticipations.

I have not time now to explain to you, as otherwise I would, how it happened that I do not possess a country house. But I may state to you in general, that it arose from my not having a large fortune, compared, I mean, with my situation, and from the peculiar duties and circumstances of my life."

"*March* 23, 1823.

"Above all remember *the one thing needful*. I had far rather that you should be a true Christian than a learned man, but I wish you to become the latter through the influence of the former. I had far rather see you unlearned than learned from the impulse of the love of human estimation as your main principle."

On the 15th of May Mr. F. Buxton moved this resolution in the House of Commons: "That the state of slavery is repugnant to the principles of the British Constitution and of the Christian Religion, and that it ought to be abolished gradually throughout the British Colonies with as much expedition as may be found consistent with a due regard to the well-being of the parties concerned." The main point was that all negro children born after a certain day were to be free.

"*May* 17, 1823.

"The debate was by no means so interesting as we expected. Buxton's opening speech was not so good as his openings have before been. His reply however, though short, was, not sweet indeed, but excellent. I was myself placed in very embarrassing circumstances from having at once to decide, without consulting my friends, on Mr. Canning's offers, if I may so term them. However, I thank God, I judged rightly, that it would not be wise to press for more on that night, as subsequent conversation with our friends rendered indubitably clear; and on the whole we have done good service, I trust, by getting Mr. Canning pledged to certain important reforms. I should speak of our gain in still stronger terms but for his (Canning's) chief friend being a West Indian, Mr. Charles Ellis, a very gentlemanly, humane man, but by no means free from the prejudices of his caste.

"Dear Robert has just been prevailed on by William's kind importunity to try to study for a while at Brompton Grove. I am glad of it on all accounts. It would add substantially to the pleasures of my life, if my dear boys could acquire firmness enough to study at home. I would do my best to promote the success of the experiment; but, believe me, it is a sad habit that of being able to study only when you have 'all appliances and means to boot.'

"I just recollect this letter will reach you on the Sunday. Allow me, therefore, to repeat my emphatic valediction *Remember*. You will be in my heart and in my prayers, and probably we shall be celebrating about the same time the memorial of our blessed Lord's suffering and the bond of the mutual affection of His disciples towards each other. The anniversaries which have passed remind me forcibly of the rapid flight of time. My course must be nearly run, though perhaps it may please that God who has hitherto caused goodness and mercy to follow me all my days, to allow me to see my dear boys entered into the exercise of their several professions, if they are several. But how glad shall I be if they all can conscientiously enter into the ministry, that most useful and most honourable of all human employments."[1]

"*June* 14.

"All may be done through prayer—almighty prayer, I am ready to say; and why not? for that it is almighty is only through the gracious ordination of the God of love and truth. Oh then, pray, pray, pray, my dearest boy. But then remember to estimate your state on self-examination not by your prayers, but by what you find to be the effects of them on your character, tempers, and life."

"*July* 12, 1823.

"It has often been a matter of grief to me

[1] Part of this letter is in the "Life of Wilberforce."

that both Henry and Robert have a sad habit of appearing, if not of being, inattentive at church. The former I have known turn half or even quite round and stare (I use the word designedly) into the opposite pew. I am not aware whether you have the same disposition (real or apparent) to inattention at public worship. I trust I need not endeavour to enforce on you that it is a practice to be watched against with the utmost care. It is not only a crime in ourselves, but it is a great stumbling-block of offence to others. The late Mr. Scott, though an excellent man, had contracted a habit of staring in general while reading the prayers of our excellent liturgy; and he once told me himself he actually did it most, when his mind was most intent on the solemn service he was performing. But to others he appeared looking at the congregation, especially at any persons entering the chapel, and many I fear were encouraged to a degree of distraction and inattention in prayer by the unseemly habit he had contracted. Now let me entreat you, my dearest boy, to watch against every approach to inattention in yourself, and to help dear Henry, in whom I have remarked the practice, to get the better of it. I have always found it a great aid in keeping my thoughts from wandering at church to repeat the prayers to myself, either in a whisper or mentally, as the minister has being going along, and I highly approve of making responses, and always when you were children tried to have you make them; but I used to think your mother did not join me in this when you were next to her, partly probably from her own mind being more closely engaged in the service—prayer being the grand means of maintaining our communication with heaven, and the life of religion in the soul claiming all possible attention."

In the next letter Wilberforce mentions that he had limited his personal expenditure so as to have larger sums to give away. He says that he had left off giving claret, then a costly wine, and some other expensive articles still exhibited by those of his rank. He speaks strongly against gratifying all the cravings of fashion, thoughtlessness, or caprice.

"BARMOUTH, *October* 14, 1823.

"MY VERY DEAR SAMUEL,—I again take up my pen to give you my sentiments on the important subject on which I promised to write to you, and on which you have kindly asked my advice. But before I proceed to fulfil this engagement let me mention what I had intended to state in my last, but omitted, that I have reason to believe dear Robert has suffered in the estimation of some of my friends, whether rightly or wrongly I really know not, from the idea that his associates were not religious men (irreligious in its common acceptation would convey more than I mean), and therefore that he preferred that class of companions. Now when people have once conceived anything of a prejudice against another, on whatever grounds, they are disposed to view all he says and does with different eyes, and to draw from it different conclusions from those which would otherwise have been produced, and I suspect dear Robert has suffered unjustly in this way. However, he will, I doubt not, live through it, and so long as all is really right, I care less for such temporary misconceptions, though, by the way, they may be very injurious to the temporal interests, and to the acceptance of the subject of them.

"But now let me state to you my sentiments concerning your principles and conduct as to society, and first I must say that if I were in your case I should be very slow in forming new acquaintances. Having already such good companions in Robert, Sir G. Prevost, and I hope Ryder, it would surely be wise to be satisfied with them at the first, unless there were any in whose instance I was sure I was on safe and good ground. But now to your question itself. There are two points of view in which this subject of good associates must naturally be regarded. The one in that which is the ordinary object of social intercourse, that I mean of recreation : for it certainly is one of the very best recreations, and may be rendered indeed not merely such, but conducive to higher and better ends. On this first head, however, I trust I need say nothing in your case, I will therefore pass it by for the present. It would, I am persuaded, be no recreation to you to be in a party which should be disgraced by obscenity or profaneness. But the second view is that which most belongs to our present inquiry—that, I mean, of the society in which it may appear necessary to take a share on grounds of conformity (where there is nothing wrong) to the ordinary customs of life, and even on the principle of 'providing things honest in the sight of all men" (honest in the Greek is δίκαιος) and not suffering your good to be evil spoken of. Now in considering this question, I am persuaded I need not begin in my dear Samuel's instance with arguing for, but may assume the principle that there are no indifferent actions properly speaking, I should rather say none with which religion has nothing to do. This however is the commonly received doctrine of those who consider themselves as very good Christians. Just as in Law it is an axiom, 'De minimis non curat lex.' On the contrary, a true Christian holds, in obedience to the injunction, 'Whatever you do in word or deed' that the desire to please his God and Saviour must be universal. It is thus that the habit of living in Christ, and to Christ is to be formed. And the difference between real and nominal Christians is more manifest on small occasions than on greater. In the latter all who do not disclaim the authority of Christ's commands must obey them, but in the former only they will apply them who do make religion their grand business, and pleasing their God and Saviour, and pleasing, instead of grieving the Spirit, their continual and habitual aim. We are therefore to decide the question of the company you should keep on Scriptural principles, and the principle I lately quoted 'Provide things honest,' &c. (There are several others of a like import, and I think they are not always sufficiently borne in mind by really good people, this of course forbids all needless singularities, &c.) That principle must doubtless be kept in view. But again, *you* will not require me to prove that it can only have any jurisdiction where there is nothing wrong to be participated in or encouraged. And therefore I am sure you will not deny that you ought not to make a part of any society in which you will be hearing what is indecent or profane. I hope that there are not many of the Oriel undergraduates from whom you would be likely to hear obscenity or profaneness, and I trust that you will not knowingly visit any such. As to the wine parties, if I have a correct idea of them they are the young men going after dinner to each other's rooms to drink their wine, eat their fruit, &c.; and with the qualification above specified, I see no reason for your absenting yourself from them, if your so doing would fairly subject you to the charge of moroseness or any other evil imputation. I understand there is no excess, and that you separate after a short time. Its being more *agreeable* to you to stay away I should not deem a legitimate motive if alone. But in all these questions the *practical* question often is, how the expenditure of any given amount of time and money (for the former I estimate full as highly as the latter) can be made productive of the best effect. There is one particular member of your college with whom I hope you will form no acquaintance. Would it make it more easy for you to avoid this, if you were able to allege that I had exacted from you a promise to that effect? It was not from Robert, but from another person, that I heard of him a particular instance of misconduct, which I believe even in the more relaxed discipline of Cambridge would have drawn on the offender exemplary punishment. Such a man must, I am sure, be a very dangerous companion. If it be necessary for you to know him, of course you will treat him like a gentleman; but further than this I hope you will not go. From what Robert said to me I have a notion that there is a very foolish practice, to call it by the softest name, of spending considerable sums in the fruit and wine of these wine drinkings, where I understood that there was no excess, every man also being allowed to please himself as to the wine he drinks. But for a young man, the son perhaps of a clergyman who is straining to the utmost to maintain him at college, stinting himself, his wife and daughters in comforts necessary to their health, for such a young man to be giving claret and buying expensive fruit for his young companions is absolutely criminal. And what is more, I will say that young men are much altered if any youth of spirit who should frankly declare, 'My father cannot afford such expensive indulgences, and I will not deprive him or my brothers and sisters for my own gratification,' would not be respected for his manliness and right feeling. Your situation is different, though, by the way, your father has left off giving claret except in some very special cases, and has entirely left off several other expensive articles, which are still exhibited by others of his rank. But then I know this will not commonly be imputed to improper parsimony in me. And if you or any other Oxonian could lighten the pressure on young men going to college, you would be rendering a highly valuable service to the community, besides the too little considered obligation of limiting our own expenditure for our own indulgence as much as we can, consistently with 'good report,' and with not suffering our good to be evil spoken of. I say this deliberately, that it is a duty not sufficiently borne in mind even by real Christians, when we read the *strong* passage in the 15th of Deuteronomy, and still more when we remember our Saviour's language in the 25th of St. Matthew, we shall see reason to be astonished that the *generality* of those who do fear God, and mean in the main to please Him, can give away so small a proportion of their fortunes, and so little appear sensible of the obligation under which they lie to economise as much as they can for the purpose of having the funds for giving away within their power. We serve a kind Master, who will even accept the will for the deed when the deed was not in our power. But this will not be held to be the case when we can gratify all the cravings of fashion and self-indulgence, or even thoughtlessness or caprice. What pleasure will a true Christian sometimes feel in sparing himself some article which he would be glad to possess, and putting the price instead into his charity purse, looking up to his Saviour and in heart offering it up to His use. Oh, my very dear Samuel, be not satisfied with the name of Christian. But strive to be a Christian 'in life and in power and in the Holy Ghost.' I think a solitary walk or ride now and then would afford an excellent opportunity for cultivating *spirituality of mind*, the grand characteristic of the thriving Christian.

"But my feelings draw me off from the proper subject I was writing upon—expense. And really, when I consider it merely in the view of the misery that may be alleviated, and the tears that may be wiped away by a very little money judiciously employed, I grow ashamed of myself for not practising more self-denial that I may apply my savings to such a purpose. Then think of the benefits to be rendered to mankind by missionary societies. Besides all this, I really believe there is commonly a special blessing on the liberal, even in this life, and on their children; and I hesitate not to say to you that, as you will, I hope, possess from me what, with the ordinary emoluments of a profession, may afford you a comfortable competence, I am persuaded I shall leave you far more likely to be happy than if you were to have inherited from me £10,000 more (and I say the same for your brothers also), the fruits of my bachelor savings. In truth, it would be so if the Word of God be true, for it is full of declarations to that effect. Now all this is general doctrine. I am aware of it. I can only give you principles here. It must be for you to apply them, and if you apply them with simplicity of intention, all, I doubt not, will be well. But again I cannot help intimating my persuasion that you would do well to confine yourself at first to the few friends you already have and on whom you can depend. And also let me suggest that it would be truly wise to be looking around you, and if you should see any one whose principles, and character, and manners are such as suggest the hope that he might be desirable even for a friend, then to cultivate his acquaintance. May our Heavenly Father direct and prosper you, carry you safely through the ordeal into which you are just about to enter, and at length receive you into that blessed world where danger will be over, and all will be love and peace and joy for evermore.

"I am ever affectionately yours,
"W. WILBERFORCE."

"*November* 5, 1823.

"I trust I scarcely need assure you that I must always wish to make you comfortable *quoad* money matters, and on the other hand that the less the cost of rendering you so, the more convenient to me. My income is much diminished within the last few years, while the expenses of my family have greatly increased. . . .

"What a comfort it is to know that our Heavenly Father is ever ready to receive all who call upon Him. He delighteth in mercy, and ever remember that as you have heard me say, mercy is kindness to the guilty, to those who deserve punishment. What a delightful consideration it is that our Saviour loves His people better than we love each other, than an earthly parent loves his child."

"*November* 7, 1823.

"There is a vile and base sentiment current among men of the world that, if you want to preserve a friend you must guard against having any pecuniary transactions with him. But it is a caution altogether unworthy of a Christian bosom. It is bottomed in the mistakenly supposed superior value of money to every other object, and in a very low estimate of human friendship. I hope I do not undervalue my money, but I prize my time at a still higher rate, and have no fear that any money transaction can ever lessen the mutual confidence and affection which subsists between us and which I trust will never be diminished. And let me take this opportunity also of stating that you would give me real pleasure by making me your friend and opening your heart to me as much in every other particular. I trust you would never find me abusing your confidence. Even any indiscretions or faults, if there should be any, if I can help to prevent your being involved in difficulties by them. But I hate to put such a case. It is no more than what is due to my dear Samuel, to say that my anticipations are of a very different sort. And I can truly declare that the good conduct and kindness of my children towards me is a source of the purest and greatest pleasure I do or can enjoy."[1]

"*August* 6, 1824.

"I can bear silence no longer, and I beg you will in future send me or your dear mother a something, be it ever so short, in the way of a letter once a week, if it be merely a certificate of your existence. I have been for some days thinking of writing to you, in consequence of my having heard that your friend Ryder and Sir George Prevost were reading classics with Mr. Keble. Could you not have been allowed to make it a triumvirate? Much as I value classical

[1] Part of this letter is in the "Life of Wilberforce."

scholarship, I prize still more highly the superior benefit to be derived from associating with such good young men as I trust the two gentlemen are whose names I have mentioned, and I have the satisfaction of knowing that you have the privilege of calling them your friends. Is it yet too late?"

"*September* 10, 1824.

"As I was talking to your mother this morning on money matters it shot across my mind that you had desired me to send you a supply, which I had neglected to do. I am truly sorry for my inadvertency, and will send you the half of a £20 bank note which I happen to possess, the other half following of course to-morrow. Ask for what you want, and we will settle when you are here. It gives me real pleasure to believe that you are economical on principle, and it is only by being so that one can be duly liberal. Without self-denial every man, be his fortune what it may, will find himself unable to act as he ought in this particular, not that *giving* is always the best charity, far from it; employing people is often a far preferable mode of serving them. To you I may say that if I have been able to be liberal not less before my marriage than after it, was from denying myself many articles which persons in my own rank of life and pecuniary circumstances almost universally indulged in. Now when I find my income considerably decreased on the one hand, and my expenses (from my four sons) greatly increased on the other, economy must even be made parsimony, which, justly construed, does not in my meaning at all exclude generosity."

This letter is here interrupted, he says, by "two young widows—both of whom had recently lost their husbands in India—with their four little children, all in deep mourning. Yet the two widows have the best of all supports in the assured persuasion that their husbands were truly pious, and in the hope that they themselves are so."

It is easy to imagine the reception given to the "two young widows" by Wilberforce. He had not yet learned the lesson of "economy or even parsimony" as regarded his charities—even when he had to reduce his expenses he spent £3,000[1] in one year on charity.

"*December* 10, 1824.

"I have deemed it quite a duty on this delicious day to prolong my country walk in a *tête-à-tête* with your dear mother, a *tête-à-tête*, however, from which our dear children's images are not excluded. I own that those who are termed Methodists by the world do give more liberally to the distressed than others, yet that I think they do not in this duty come up to the full demands of Scripture. The great mistake

---

[1] A single year's almsgiving exceeded £3,000. "Life of Bishop Wilberforce," vol. i. p. 22.

that prevails as I conceive is, it's being thought right that all persons who are received on the footing of gentlemen are to live alike. And without economy there cannot be sufficient liberality. I can sincerely declare that my wish that my sons should be economical, which is quite consistent with being generous, nay, as I said before, is even necessary to it, arises far more from my conviction of the effects of economical habits on their minds and happiness in future life, than on account of the money that will be thereby saved. You have heard me, I doubt not, praise Paley's excellent remark on the degree in which a right constitution of the habits tends to produce happiness, and you may proceed with the train of ideas I have called up in your mind."

"*October* 26, 1825.

"You ask me about your Uncle Stephen's having been a newspaper reporter. He was. The case was this. At the age of, I believe, eighteen, he came up to town to study the law, when the sudden death of his father not only stopped his supplies, but threw on his hands the junior branches of the family, more especially three or four sisters. Seeing no other resource, he embraced an offer, made to him I believe through or by Mr. Richardson, the friend of poor Sheridan. Richardson afterwards came into Parliament, and the fact respecting Stephen came out thus, a few years ago. A regulation was proposed by some of the benchers of Lincoln's Inn that no one should be permitted to be called to the Bar who ever had practised the reporting art. Sheridan brought the question forward in the House of Commons. Stephen, who was then in Parliament, spoke to the question, and in arguing against the illiberal and even cruel severity of the regulation, put a supposed case, that the son of a gentleman, by a father's sudden death was at once deprived of the means of pursuing the legal profession on which he was just entering, being also harassed in his mind by the distressed state of some affectionate sisters. Thus embarrassed, he received an offer of employment as a reporter, and gladly accepted it and discharged its duties, thereby being enabled to prosecute his professional studies as well as to assist his relatives. 'But,' added Stephen, 'the case I have just stated is no imaginary one. It is the story of a living individual. It is that, sir, of the individual who has now the honour to address you.' There is in all bodies of Englishmen a generous feeling which is always called forth powerfully when a man confesses, or rather boldly avows any circumstance respecting himself which, according to the false estimate of the world, might be supposed to disparage him; as when Peel at the meeting for a monument to James Watt declared that, 'owing all his prosperity to the successful industry of a person originally in the humble walks of life,' the applause was overpowering. And I never remember a more general or louder acclamation than immediately broke out when Stephen had (indeed before he had completely) closed his declaration."

"*December* 16, 1825.

"It is Henry Thornton[1] that was connected with the house of Pole & Co. He became a partner about five months ago. The storm through which he has been passing has been indeed violent; but the call for self-possession, temper, judgment, and above all scrupulous, punctilious integrity has been abundantly answered. He has behaved so as to draw on him the universal applause of all who have witnessed his conduct. Mr. Jno. Smith especially speaks of it in the highest terms, and has been acting towards him with corresponding generosity and kindness. It has been very strikingly evidenced that commercial transactions on a great scale enlarge the mind, and the obedience which, with men of real principle, is paid to the point of mercantile honour, produces a habit of prompt, decisive integrity in circumstances of embarrassment and distress. I am happy to be able to tell you that there is reason to

[1] Eldest son of Wilberforce's old friend and ally, Henry Thornton, of Battersea Rise, who died in 1815. The Henry Thornton of the text was only twenty-five years old when this letter was written.

believe that while Henry will gain great credit he will lose no money. He has borne the trial with the calmness of a veteran."

"*Sunday, January* 22, 1826.

"You may have heard me mention, that when in my solitary bachelor state I was alone all day on the Sunday, I used after dinner to call up before me the images of my friends and acquaintances, and to consider how I could benefit or gratify them. And when the mind is scarcely awake, or, at least, active enough for any superior purpose, this is no bad employment for a part of the day, especially if practised with religious associations and purposes. The day is so raw here that I have yielded to your mother's kind entreaties that I would not go to church, where the greater part of the family now is at afternoon service. So I am glad to spend a part of my day with my dearest Samuel.

"I will remind you of an idea which I threw out on the day preceding your departure—that I feared I had scarcely enough endeavoured to impress on my children the idea that they must as Christians be a peculiar people. I am persuaded that you cannot misunderstand me to mean that I wish you to affect singularity in indifferent matters. The very contrary is our duty. But from that very circumstance of its being right that we should be like the rest of the world in exterior, manners, &c., &c., results an augmentation of the danger of our not maintaining that diversity, nay, that contrast, which the Eye of God ought to see in us to the worldly way of thinking and feeling on all the various occasions of life, and in relation to its various interests. The man of the world considers religion as having nothing to do with 99-100ths of the affairs of life, considering it as a medicine and not as his food, least of all as his refreshment and cordial. He naturally takes no more of it than his health requires. How opposite this to the apostle's admonition, 'Whatever ye do in word or deed, do all in the name of the Lord Jesus, giving thanks to God the Father through Him.' This is being spiritually-minded, and being so is truly declared to be life and peace. By the way, if you do not possess that duodecimo volume, 'Owen on Spiritual Mindedness,' let me beg you to get and read it carefully. There are some obscure and mystic passages, but much that I think is likely to be eminently useful; and may our Heavenly Father bless to you the perusal of it. . . ."

"*February* 27, 1826.

"Let me assure you that you give me great pleasure by telling me unreservedly any doubts you may entertain of the propriety of my principles or conduct. I love your considering and treating me as a friend, and I trust you will never have reason to regret your having so done, either in relation to your benefit or your comfort. In stating my suspicions that I had not sufficiently endeavoured to impress on my children, and that you were scarcely enough aware of the force of the dictum that Christians were to be a peculiar people, I scarcely need assure you that I think the commands, 'Provide things honest in the sight of all men, whatever things are lovely, whatsoever of good report,' &c. (admirably illustrated and enforced by St. Paul's account of his own principles of becoming all things to all men), clearly prove that so far from being needlessly singular, we never ought to be so, but for some special and good reason. Again, I am aware of what you suggest that, in our days, in which the number of those who profess a stricter kind of religion than the world of *soi-disant* Christians in general, there is danger lest a party spirit should creep in with its usual effects and evils. Against this, therefore, we should be on the watch. And yet, though not enlisting ourselves in a party, we ought, as I think you will admit, to assign considerable weight to any opinions or practices which have been sanctioned by the authority of good men in general. As again, you will I think admit, that in any case in which the more advanced Christians and the less advanced are both affected, the former and their interests deserve more of our consideration than the latter. For instance, it is alleged in behalf of certain worldly compliances, that by making them you will give a favourable idea, produce a pleasing impression of your religious principles, and dispose people the rather to adopt them. But then, if you thereby are likely to become an *offence* (in the Scripture sense) to weaker Christians, (persons, with all their infirmities, eminently dear to Christ,) you may do more harm than good, and that to the class which had the stronger claim to your kind offices. Let my dear Samuel think over the topic to which I was about next to proceed. I mean our Saviour's language to the Laodicean Church expressing His abhorrence and disgust at lukewarmness, and the danger of damping the religious affections by such recreations as He had in mind. Of course I don't object to domestic dances. It is not the act, the *saltus*, but the *whole tone* of an assembly."

"CLIFTON, *May* 27, 1826.

"I am very glad to think that you will be with us. Your dear mother's spirits are not always the most buoyant, and, coming first to reside in a large, new house without having some of her children around her, would be very likely to infuse a secret melancholy which might sadden the whole scene, and even produce, by permanent association, a lasting impression of despondency. I finish this letter after hearing an excellent sermon from

Robert Hall. It was not merely an exhibition of powerful intellect, but of fervent and feeling piety, especially impressing on his hearers to live by the faith of the love of Christ daily, habitually looking to Him in all His characters. Prayer, prayer, my dear Samuel; let your religion consist much in prayer. May you be enabled more and more to walk by faith and not by sight, to feel habitually as well as to recognise in all your more deliberate calculations and plans, that the things that are seen are temporal, but the things that are not seen are eternal. Then you will live above the world, as one who is waiting for the coming of the Lord Jesus Christ." [1]

"*April* 20, 1826.

" I would gladly fill my sheet, yet I can prescribe what may do almost as well. Shut your door and muse until you fancy me by your side, and then think what I should say to you, which I dare say your own mind would supply."

"*September* 30.

"I am thankful to reflect that at the very moment I am now thinking of you and addressing you; you also are probably engaged in some religious exercise, solitary or social (for I was much gratified by learning from a passage in one of your letters to your mother that you and Anderson went through

[1] The beginning of this letter is in the "Life of Wilberforce."

the service of our beautiful liturgy together). Perhaps you are thinking of your poor old father, and, my dear boy, I hope you often pray for me, and I beg you will continue to do so.

"I am not sure whether or not I told you of our having been for a week at Lea,[1] having been detained there by my being slightly indisposed. But it was worth while to be so, if it were only to witness, or rather to experience, Lady Anderson's exceeding kindness. I really do not recollect having ever before known such high merits and accomplishments—the pencil and music combined with such unpretending humility, such true simplicity and benevolence. With these last Sir Charles is also eminently endowed. He reads his family prayers with great feeling, and especially with a reverence which is always particularly pleasing to me. There is, in 'Jonathan Edwards on the Religious Affections,' a book from which you will, I think, gain much useful matter, a very striking passage, in which he condemns with great severity, but not at all too great, *me judice*, that familiarity with the Supreme King which was affected by some of the religionists of his day, as well as by Dr. Hawker recently, and remarks very truly that Moses and

---

[1] Lea, Lincolnshire—the residence of Sir C. and Lady Anderson. The son, in his turn, Sir Charles Anderson, was Bishop Wilberforce's life-long friend.

Elijah, and Abraham the friend of God (and all of them honoured by such especial marks of the Divine condescension), always manifested a holy awe and reverence when in the Divine presence."

Samuel Wilberforce had written to his father asking him what advice he should give to a friend whose family was very irreligious. In the house of this friend 'it was a common phrase accompanying a shake of each other's hands on meeting, "May we meet together in *hell*."' The answer to the appeal for advice is as follows:—

"*July* 28, 1826.

"I will frankly confess to you that the clearness and strength of the command of the apostle, 'Children, obey your parents in all things' (though in one passage it is added, 'in the Lord') weighed so strongly with me as to lead me, at first, to doubt whether or not it did not overbalance all opposing considerations and injunctions, yet more reflection has brought me to the conclusion, to which almost all those whom I consulted came still more promptly, that it is the duty of your young friend to resist his parents' injunction to go to the play or the opera. That they are quite hotbeds of vice no one, I think, can deny, for much more might be said against them than is contained in my 'Practical View,' though I own the considerations there stated appear to my understanding such as must to any one who means to act on Christian principles be perfectly decisive. One argument against the young man's giving up the point in these instances, which has great weight with me, is this, that he must either give himself entirely up to his friends and suffer them at least to dictate to him his course of conduct, or make a stand somewhere. Now I know not what ground he will be likely to find so strong as this must be confessed to be, by all who will argue the question with him on Scriptural principles, and more especially on those I have suggested in my 'Practical View' of the love of God, and I might have added, that of the apostle's injunction, 'Whatever ye do in word or deed, do all in the name of the Lord Jesus, giving thanks to God and the Father through Him.' I scarcely need remark that the refusal should be rendered as unobjectionable as possible by the modest and affectionate manner of urging it, and by endeavouring to render the whole conduct and demeanour doubly kind and assiduous. I well remember that when first it pleased God to touch my heart, now rather above forty years ago, it had been reported of me that I was deranged, and various other rumours were propagated to my disadvantage. It was under the cloud of these prejudices that I presented myself to some old friends, and spent some time with them (after the close of the session) at Scarborough. I conversed and behaved in the spirit above recommended, and I was careful to embrace any little opportunity of pleasing them (little presents often have no small effects), and I endeavoured to impress them with a persuasion that I was not less happy than before. The consequence was all I could desire, and I well recollect that the late Mrs. Henry Thornton's mother, a woman of very superior powers and of great influence in our social circle, one day broke out to my mother—she afterwards said to me something of the same kind, not without tears—'Well, I can only say if *he* is deranged I hope we all shall become so.' To your young friend again I need not suggest the duty of constant prayer for his nearest relatives. By degrees they will become softened, and he will probably enjoy the delight of finding them come over to the blessed path he is himself pursuing. He will also find that self-denial, and a disposition to subject himself to any trouble or annoyance in order to promote his friends' comfort, or exemption from some grievance, will have a very powerful effect in conciliating his friends. With all the courtesy that prevails in high life, no one, I think, can associate with those who move in it, without seeing how great a share selfishness has in deciding their language and conduct, saving themselves trouble or money, &c., &c. Happily the objections of worldly parents to their children becoming religious are considerably weakened since it has pleased God to diffuse serious religion so much through the higher ranks in society: they no longer despair, as they once did, of their sons and daughters not forming any eligible matrimonial alliance or any respectable acquaintances or friendships. The grand blessing of acting in the way I recommend is the peace of conscience it is likely to produce. There are, we know, occasions to which our Saviour's words must apply, 'He that loveth father and mother more than Me is not worthy of Me,' and I doubt not that if your friend does the violence to his natural feelings which the case supposes, in the spirit of faith and prayer, he will be rewarded even by a present enjoyment of spiritual comfort. If I mistake not I wrote to you lately on the topic of the joy which Christians ought to find familiar to them, still more the peace; and the course he would pursue would, I believe, be very likely to ensure the possession of them. We have been, and still are, highly gratified by finding true religion establishing itself more and more widely. Lord Mandeville, whose parent stock on both sides must be confessed to be as unfavourable as could be well imagined in this highly favoured country, is truly in earnest. He, you may have forgot, married Lady Olivia's only daughter. He is a man of very good sense; though having been destined to the Navy, which had been for generations a family service, his education was probably not quite such as one would wish. He is a man of the greatest simplicity of character, only rather too quiet and silent."

"HIGHWOOD HILL,
"*November 27*, 1826.

"I hope you are pleased, I assure you I am, with the result of your B.A. course. And I scarcely dare allow myself to wish that you may be in the 1st class, or at least to wish it with any degree of earnestness or still less of anxiety. The Almighty has been so signally kind to me even in my worldly affairs, and so much more gracious than I deserved in my domestic concerns, that it would indicate a heart never to be satisfied were I not disposed in all that concerns my children, to cast all my care on Him: indeed, you pleased me not a little by stating your persuasion that it *might be* better for you ultimately not to have succeeded (to the utmost) on this very occasion. And I rejoice the more in this impression of yours, because I am sure it does not in your instance arise from the want of feeling; from that cold-blooded and torpid temperament that often tends to indolence, and if it sometimes saves its proprietor a disappointment, estranges him from many who might otherwise attach themselves to him, and shuts him out from many sources of pure and virtuous pleasure.

"Your dear mother in all weather that is not bad enough to drive the labourers within doors, is herself *sub dio*, studying the grounds, giving directions for new walks, new plantations, flower-beds, &c. And I am thankful for being able to say that the exposure to cold and dew hitherto has not hurt her —perhaps it has been beneficial."

"*August* 25, 1827.

"I was lately looking into Wrangham's 'British Biography,' and I was forcibly struck by observing that by far the larger part of the worthies the work commemorates were carried off before they reached to the age I have attained to. And yet, as I think, I must have told you, Dr. Warren, the first medical authority of that day, declared in 1788 that I could not then last above two or three weeks, not so much from the violence of an illness from which I had then suffered, as from the utter want of stamina. Yet a gracious Providence has not only spared my life, but permitted me to see several of my dear children advancing into life, and you, my dear Samuel, as well as Robert, about to enter into Holy Orders so early that if it should please God to spare my life for about a couple of years, which according to my present state of health seems by no means improbable, I may have the first and great pleasure of witnessing your performance of the sacred service of the Church. It is little in me—I mean a very ordinary proof of my preference of spiritual to earthly things, of my desiring to walk rather by faith than by sight—that I rejoice in the prospect of your becoming a clergyman rather than a lawyer, which appeared the alternative in your instance; but it is due to you, my dear Samuel, to say that it is a very striking proof of your having been enabled by, I humbly trust, the highest of all influences, to form this decision, when from your talents and qualifications it appeared by no means improbable that in the legal line you might not improbably rise into the enjoyment of rank and affluence. It is but too true that my feelings would, at your time of life, have been powerfully active in another direction. Perhaps this very determination may have been in part produced by that connection to which you look forward. And may it please God, my dear Samuel, to grant you the desire of your heart in this particular and to render the union conducive to your spiritual benefit and that of your partner also, so that it may be looked back upon with gratitude even in a better world, as that which has tended not only to your mutual happiness during the journey of life, but has contributed to bring you both after its blessed termination to the enjoyment of the rest that remaineth for the people of God."

This letter refers to Samuel Wilberforce's marriage with Emily Sargent, as to which his father remarks:

"Viewed in a worldy light, the connection cannot be deemed favourable to either of you."

"*March* 20, 1828.

"The cheerfulness, which at an earlier period of my life might have been a copious spring supplying my letters with a stream of pleasant sentiments and feelings, has been chilled even to freezing by advancing years, and yet, to do myself justice, though this may have dulled the activity and liveliness of my epistles, I think it has not cooled the kindly warmth of heart with which I write to my friends and least of all to my children."

"*July* 22, 1828.

"I am glad that any opportunity for your coming forward as a public speaker has occurred, I mean an opportunity proper for you to embrace, in which you were rather a drawn (though not a pressed) man and not a volunteer. We have had the great pleasure of having dear Robert officiate twice, both in the reading-desk and the pulpit. The apparent, as well as real, simplicity of his whole performance must have impressed every observant and feeling hearer with a very favourable view of his character. His language remarkably simple, much every way in his sermon to esteem and love. It suggested one or two important topics for consideration, which I shall be glad to talk over with you hereafter, as well as with Robert himself. One is, whether he did not fall into what I have often thought an error in the sermons of sound divines, and in those perhaps of Oxonians more than Cantabs—that I mean of addressing their congregations as being all real Christians—children of God, &c.—who needed (to use our Saviour's figure in John xiii.) only to have their feet washed. Whatever may be the right doctrinal opinion as to baptismal regeneration, all really orthodox men will grant, I presume, that as people grow up they may lose that privilege of being children of God which we trust they who were baptised in their infancy did enjoy, and would have reaped the benefit of it had they died before, by the gradual development of their mental powers, they became moral agents capable of responsibility. And if so, should not their particular sins of disposition, temper, or conduct be used rather to convince them of their being in a sinful state, and as therefore requiring the converting grace of God, than as merely wanting a little reformation?"

"*November* 20, 1828.

"Has Sargent[1] heard of the fresh explosion in the British and Foreign Bible Society? I truly and deeply regret it. It has proceeded from a proposal to print the Septuagint. In the discussion that took place on that topic it was perhaps unwarily

[1] The Rev. John Sargent, of Lavington, father of Mrs. Samuel Wilberforce.

said there was no proper standard of the Holy Scriptures. No standard!!!!! Then we have no Bible! You see how a little Christian candour would have prevented this rupture. Oh that they would all remember that the end of the commandment is Love. I fear this is not the test by which in our days Christians are to be ascertained: may we all cultivate in ourselves this blessed principle and pray for it more earnestly. I am quite pleased myself, Robert is delighted, by the appointment to the Professorship (Hebrew) of Pusey—above £1,200 per annum. Pusey had opposition, and is appointed by the Duke of Wellington, solely we suppose on the ground of superior merit."

"*February* 20, 1829.

"Legh Richmond,[1] though an excellent man, was not a man of refinement or of taste. I cannot deny the justice of your remarks as far as I can fairly allow myself to form a judgment without referring to the book. I entirely concur in your censure of Richmond's commonplace, I had almost termed it profane, way in which he speaks of the Evil Spirit. This falls under the condemnation justly pronounced by Paley against levity in religion.

"When I can spare a little eyesight or time, I feel myself warranted to indulge the pleasure I always have in the exercise of the domestic affections,

[1] His life had been recently published.

and in gratifying you (as I hope it is not vanity to think I do) in writing to you at a time when you are in circumstances of more quiet than usual, though I am aware that a man of your age, who is spending his first year of married life with a partner, between whom and himself there was great mutual attachment, grounded on esteem, and a mutual acquaintance with each other's characters and dispositions, can never be so happy as when he is enjoying a *tête-à-tête* with his bride. By the way, do you keep anything in the nature of a journal? A commonplace book I take it for granted you keep; and speaking of books, let me strongly urge you to keep your accounts regularly, and somewhat at least in the mode in which we keep ours—under different heads. If you have not the plan, tell me and I will send it to you. Its excellence is that it enables you with ease to see how your money goes; and remember we live in days in which a single sovereign given by an individual is often productive of great effects. Where is it that a single drop (stalactite) from a roof, falling into the ocean, is made to bemoan itself on being lost in the abyss of waters, when afterwards it became the seminal principle of the great pearl that constituted the glory of the Great Mogul? And now also, remember the Church Missionary Society is so poor, that it will be compelled to quit some fields whitening to the harvest, unless it can have its funds considerably augmented."

SAMUEL WILBERFORCE, Aged 29.

The next letter refers to the offer of the vicarage of Ribchester, near Preston, in Lancashire, made by the Bishop of Chester to Samuel Wilberforce.

"*March* 3, 1829.

"Whether regarded in relation to your bodily strength, your spiritual interests, or to prudence in affairs, I should be disposed to advise you to decline, with a due sense of kindness, &c., the Bishop's offer. Your constitution is not a strong one, and it is highly desirable in that view alone that you should for a time officiate in a small sphere, and if it may be in a place where, as from your vicinity to Oxford, you can have assistance when you are not equal yourself to the whole duty. With such a scattered population, there must be a call I conceive for great bodily strength. Secondly, the situation appears to me still less eligible considered on higher grounds. It is no ground of blame to you that your studies have not hitherto been of divinity. Supply all that I should say under that head, were I not writing to one who is capable himself of suggesting it to his own mind. Again, you cannot have that acquaintance with human nature, either in general, or in your own self, which it would be desirable for any one to possess who was to be placed in so wide and populous a field, especially in one so circumstanced as this particular place. Then you would be at a distance from almost all your friends, which I mention now in reference to the spiritual disadvantages of the situation, not in relation to your comfort and Emily's, in which, however, it may be fairly admitted to some weight. Again, *I* should much regret your being placed where you would naturally be called to study controversial anti-Roman Catholic divinity, rather than that which expects the cultivation of personal holiness in yourself and your parishioners. I could say much on this head. Thirdly, Mr. Neale sees the objections on the ground of pecuniary interest, as alone of so much weight, as to warrant your refusing the offer—a vicarage. Its income is commonly derived from small payments, and in that district probably of poor people whom you would not, could not squeeze, and yet without squeezing from whom you probably would get nothing. Most likely a curate would be indispensable."

On the same topic Wilberforce writes again:—

"*March 17th*, 1829.

"I ought to tell you that in the reasons I assigned to the Bishop for declining his offer, one, and in itself perhaps the strongest, (nay, certainly so, not perhaps,) was my persuasion that for any one educated and associated as you have been, it was of very great importance with a view to your spiritual state, (more especially for the cultivation of devotional feelings and spirituality of mind,) that he should in the outset of his ministerial course be for some time in a quiet and retired situation, where he could live in the enjoyment of domestic comfort, of leisure for religious reading and meditation, and devotional exercises; while, on the contrary, it was very undesirable in lieu of these to be placed in circumstances in which he would almost necessarily be almost incessantly arguing for Protestant principles—in short, would be occupied in the religion of the head rather than of the heart. I own to you in confidence (though I believe I shall make the avowal to my dear Robert himself) that I am sometimes uneasy on a ground somewhat congenial with this, about the tutor of Oriel. For though I doubt not the solidity of his religious character, yet I fear his situation is far from favourable to the growth in grace, and would, alas! need every help we can have for the advancement of personal religion within us, and can scarcely bear without injury any circumstances that have an unfavourable tendency. I trust my dear Samuel will himself consider that he is now responsible for living in circumstances peculiarly favourable to the growth of personal piety, and therefore that he should use his utmost endeavours to derive the benefits that appear, (humanly speaking,) to be placed within his reach. Oh, my dearest boy, we are all too sadly lukewarm, sadly too little urging forward with the earnestness that might justly be expected from those that are contending for an incorruptible crown. Did you ever read Owen on spiritual-mindedness? There are some passages that to me appear almost unintelligible (one at least), but it is in the main, I think, a highly useful book. I need not say how sorry we are to hear of Emily being poorly. But our gourds must have something to alloy their sweets. D. G. your mother is recovering gradually, and now profits much from a jumbling pony-chair; its shaking quality renders its value to her double what it would be otherwise."[1]

"*March* 19, 1829.

"In speaking of Whately's book I ought to have said that I had not got to the part in which he speaks of imputed righteousness. I remember it was an objection made to my 'Practical View' by a certain strange head of a college that I was silent on that point. The honest truth is, I never considered it. I have always been disposed to believe it to be in some sort true, but not to deem it a matter of importance, if the doctrine of free grace and justification by faith be held, which are, I believe, of primary importance. Hooker, unless I forget, is clearly for it; see his sermon on Justification. I trust I need not fear your misconstruing

[1] The first few lines of this letter are in the "Life of Bishop Wilberforce."

me, and supposing I can be advising you, either to be roguish, or shabbily reserved. But really I do think that you may produce an unfavourable and false impression of your principles and professional character, by talking unguardedly about *Methodistical* persons and opinions. Mrs. R. may report you as UNSOUND to the Bishop of Winchester, and he imbibe a prejudice against you. Besides, my dear Samuel, I am sure you will not *fire* when I say that you may see reason on farther reading, and reflection, and more experience to change or qualify some of the opinions you may now hold. I own, (I should not be honest if I did not say so,) that I think I have myself witnessed occasions which have strengthened with me the impression that you may need this hint. . . . Have you any parishioners who have been used to hear Methodists or Dissenters, or have you any who appear to have had, or still to have, much feeling of religion? I cannot help suspecting that it is a mistaken notion that the lower orders are to be chiefly instructed in the ordinary practical duties of religion, whereas I own I believe them to be quite capable of impressions on their affections: on the infinite love of their God and Redeemer, and of their corresponding obligation to Love and Obedience. We found peasants more open to attacks on their consciences, on the score of being wanting in gratitude, than on any other."

"*April* 3, 1829.

"Articles sent to Mr. Samuel—Bewick, Venn's Sermons (2 vols.), White's 'Selborne' (2 vols. bound in one), 2nd vol. of 'The Monastery.' A lending library is, I think, likely to be considerably beneficial. It cannot but have a tendency to generate in the poor a disposition favourable to domestic habits and pleasures, and to seek their enjoyments at home rather than in the alehouse, and it strikes me as likely to confirm this taste, to encourage the poor people's children to read to them. Send me a list of any books you will like to have for your lending library, and I will by degrees pick them up for you. . . .

"We ought to be always making it our endeavour to be experiencing peace and joy in believing, and that we do not enjoy more of this sunshine of the breast is, I fear, almost always our own fault. We ought not to acquiesce quietly in the want of them, whereas we are too apt to be satisfied if our consciences do not reproach us with anything wrong, if we can on good grounds entertain the persuasion that we are safe; and we do not sufficiently consider that we serve a gracious and kind master who is willing that we should taste that He is gracious. Both in St. John's first general Epistle, and in our Lord's declaration in John xv., we are assured that our Lord's object and the apostles' in telling us of our having spiritual supplies and communion, is that our joy may be full. It is a great comfort to me to reflect that you are in circumstances peculiarly favourable to your best interests. To be spiritually-minded is both life and peace. How much happier would your dear mother be if she were living the quiet life you and Emily do, instead of being cumbered about many things; yet she is in the path of duty, and that is all in all."

"*September* 7, 1829.

"An admirable expedient has this moment suggested itself to me, which will supersede the necessity for my giving expression to sentiments and feelings, for which you will give me full credit, though unexpressed. It is that of following the precedent set by a candidate for the City of Bristol in conjunction with Mr. Burke. The latter had addressed his electors in a fuller effusion of eloquence than was used to flow even from his lips, when his colleague, conscious that he should appear to great disadvantage were he to attempt a speech, very wisely confined himself to, 'Gentlemen, you have heard Mr. Burke's excellent speech. I say ditto to the whole of it.' Sure I am that no language of mine could give you warmer or more sincere assurances of parental affection than you will have received in the letter of your dear mother, which she has just put into my hands to be inserted into my letter. To all she has said, therefore, I say ditto. My dear Samuel, I must tell you the pleasure with which I look back on what I witnessed at Checkendon,[1] and how it combines with, and augments the joyful gratulations with which I welcome the 7th of September.[2] I hope I am deeply thankful to the bountiful Giver of all good for having granted me in you a son to whose future course I can look with so much humble hope, and even joyful confidence. It is also with no little thankfulness that I reflect on your domestic prospects, from the excellent qualities of your, let me say *our*, dear Emily. I must stop, the rest shall be prayer, prayer for both of you, that your course in this life may be useful and honourable, and that you may at length, accompanied by a large assemblage of the sheep of Christ, whom you have been the honoured instrument of bringing to the fold of Christ, have an abundant entrance into the everlasting kingdom of God."

"*September* 28, 1829.

"How much do they lose of comfort, as well as, I believe, in incentives to gratitude and love, and if it be not their own fault thereby in the means of practical improvement, who do not accustom themselves to watch the operations of the Divine Hand.

[1] Checkendon, on the Chiltern Hills in Oxfordshire, Samuel Wilberforce's first curacy, where his memory was long cherished.
[2] Samuel's birthday.

I have often thought that, had it not been for the positive declarations of the Holy Scriptures concerning the attention of the Almighty Governor of the universe to our minutest comforts and interests enforced by a comparison with the στοργή of parental affection, we should not dare to be so presumptuous as to believe, that He who rolls the spheres along, would condescend thus to sympathise with our feelings, and attend to our minutest interests. Here also Dr. Chalmers' suggestions, derived from the discoveries made to us through the microscope, come in to confirm the same delightful persuasion. I am persuaded that many true Christians lose much pleasure they might otherwise enjoy from not sufficiently watching the various events of their lives, more especially in those little incidents, as we rather unfitly term them; for, considering them as links in the chain, they maintain the continuity, as much as those which we are apt to regard as of greater size and consequence."

"*November* 21, 1829.

"We have been for a few days at Battersea Rise. But your mother will, I doubt not, have told you the memorabilia of this visit, and especially the inexhaustible conversational powers of Sir James Mackintosh. I wish I may be able, some time or other, to enable you to hear these powers exerted. Poor fellow! he is, however, the victim of his own social dispositions and excellences. For I cannot but believe, that the superfluous hours dissipated in these talks, might suffice for the performance of a great work. They are to him, what, alas! in some degree, my letters were to me during my Parliamentary life, and even to this day."

"*December* 17, 1829.

"We ought not to expect this life to flow on smoothly without rubs or mortification. Indeed, it is a sentiment which I often inculcate on myself that, to use a familiar phrase, we here have more than our bargain, as Christians, in the days in which we live; for I apprehend the promise of the life that now is, combined with that which is to come, was meant to refer rather to mental peace and comfort, than to temporal prosperity. My thoughts have been of late often led into reflections on the degree in which we are wanting to ourselves, in relation to the rich and bright prospects set before us as attainable in the Word of God. More especially I refer to that of the Christian's hope and peace and joy. Again and again we are assured that joy is ordinarily and generally to be the portion of the Christian. Yet how prone are but too commonly those, whom we really believe to be entitled to the name of Christians, disposed to remain contented without the possession of this delightful state of heart; and to regard it as the privilege of some rarely gifted, and eminently favoured Christians, rather than as the general character of all, yet I believe that except for some hypochondriacal affection, or state of spirits arising from bodily ailments, every Christian ought to be very distrustful of himself, *and to call himself to account, as it were*, if he is not able to maintain a settled frame of 'inward peace,' if not joy. It is to be obtained through the Holy Spirit, and therefore when St. Paul prays for the Roman Christians that they may be filled with all *peace* and *joy* in believing, and may abound in hope, it is added, through the power of the Holy Ghost."

"HIGHWOOD HILL,
"*December* 31, 1829.

"MY DEAR CHILDREN,—For to both of you I address myself. An idea, which for so old a fellow as myself you will allow somewhat to be deserving the praise of brightness, has just struck my mind, and I proceed to act upon it. Are you Yorkshireman enough to know the article (an excellent one it is) entitled a Christmas, or sometimes a goose or a turkey pie? Its composition is this. Take first the smallest of eatable birds, as a snipe, for instance, then put it within its next neighbour of the feathered race, I mean in point of size, the woodcock, insert the two into a teal, the teal into a duck, the duck and Co. into a fowl, the fowl into a goose, the goose and Co. into a turkey. In imitation of this laudable precedent, I propose, though with a variation, as our Speaker would say, in the order of our proceeding, that this large sheet which I have selected for the purpose should contain the united epistles of all the family circle, from the fullest grown if not largest in dimensions, myself, to the most dimunitive, little William.[1] As the thought is my own, I will begin the execution of it, and if any vacant space should remain, I will fill it, just as any orifices left vacant in said pie are supplied by the pouring in of the jelly. But I begin to be ashamed of this jocoseness when I call to mind on what day I am writing—the day which, combined with the succeeding one, the 1st of January, I consider, except perhaps my birthday, as the most important of the whole year. For a long period (as long as I lived in the neighbourhood of the Lock, or rather not far from it) I used to receive the Sacrament, which was always administered there on New Year's Day. And the heart must be hard and cold, which that sacred ordinance in such a relation, would not soften and warm into religious sensibility and tenderness. I was naturally led into looking backwards to the past days of my life, and forward to the future; led to consider in what pleasant places my lines were fallen,

[1] Only son of Wilberforce's eldest son William.

how goodly was my heritage, that the bounds of my life should be fixed in that little spot, in which, of the whole earth, there has been the greatest measure of temporal comforts, and of spiritual privileges. That it should be also in the eighteenth century, for where should I have been, a small, weakly man, had I been born either among our painted or skin-clothed ancestors, or in almost any other before or after it? As they would have begun by exposing me, there need be no more inquiry as to the sequel of the piece. Next take my station in life, neither so high as naturally to intoxicate me, nor so low as to excite to envy or degradation. Take then the other particulars of my condition, both personal and circumstantial. But I need go no farther, but leave it to you to supply the rest. And you will likewise, I doubt not, pursue the same mental process in your own instance also, and find, as may well be the case, that the retrospect and prospect afford abundant matter for gratitude and humiliation, (I am sure I find the latter most powerfully called forth in my heart by my own survey). Many thanks for your last kind letter. You have precisely anticipated what was said by the several *dramatis personæ*. It is a real sacrifice for Emily and you to be absent from my family circle. But the sacrifice is to duty, and that is enough. And you have no small ground for comfort, from your not having to go through the 'experiment solitary,' as Lord Bacon terms it, but to have one, to whom you may say that solitude is sweet. But I must surrender the pen to your dear mother."

The country was at that time extremely disturbed by what were known as the "Swing Riots."[1] Bands of rioters went about, burning ricks and threshing machines, then newly introduced, and considered by the labourers as depriving them of the winter threshing work. Wilberforce seems to have shared this feeling.

"Highwood Hill,
"*November* 25, 1830.

"Your mother suggests that a threshing machine used to be kept in one of your barns. If so I really think it should be removed. I should be very sorry to have it stated that a threshing machine had been burnt on the premises of the Rev. Samuel Wilberforce; they take away one of the surest sources of occupation for farmers in frost and snow times. In what a dreadful state the country now is! Gisborne, I find, has stated his opinion, that the present is the period of pouring out the 7th Vial, when there was to be general confusion, insubordination, and misery. It really appears in the political world, like what the abolition of some of the great elements in

[1] The leader of these riots, whose exact personality is unknown, was called "Jack Swing," and in this name the mob sent their threats and summonses.

the physical world would be; the extinction, for instance, of the principle of gravity."

"*December* 9, 1830.

"I have been delaying the books that all might go together. Mather's 'Magnalia'[1] shall be one of them. There is a very curious passage in it early in the volume, in which in Charles I's time, he says, expenses have been increasing so much of late years that men can no longer maintain their rank in society. Assuredly this Government is greatly to be preferred before the last. Brougham better than Copley, and several highly respectable besides, the Grants (Charles is in the Cabinet), Lord Althorp, Sir James Graham, Lord Grey himself, highly respectable as family men; Denman a very honest fellow. The worst appointment is Holland, Duchy of Lancaster; he has much church patronage which, though I love the man, I cannot think decorous. Lord Lansdowne, very decent, Lord Goderich ditto. But your mother is worrying me all this time to force me out, and Joseph declares the letters will be too late. So farewell."

"*December* 17, 1830.

"I have always thought that your having a

---

[1] "Magnalia Christi Americana, or Ecclesiastical History of New England," by Cotton Mather, D.D. It was a costly book with a large map. Southey considered it one of the most "singular books in this or any other language."

strong virtuous attachment when you first went to the University was a great security to you. The blessed effects of this safeguard we shall one day know. It will be a mutual augmentation of attachment and happiness to find that those whom we loved best had been rendered the instruments more or less of our salvation. . . .

"That religious feelings are contagious (if I may use the word so), is undeniable, and there may be temporary accesses of religious feeling, which may produce a temporary effervescence, with little or none of the real work of God on the heart. But you and I, who are not Calvinists, believe that even where the influence of the Holy Spirit was in the heart, that Spirit may be grieved and quenched. The good seed in the hearts of the stony-ground hearers is just an instance in point. When my friend Terrot was chaplain, of the *Defence* I think, great numbers of the rough sailors were deeply affected by his conversation and sermons, of whom, I think he said, thirty only appeared in the sequel to be permanently changed."

"*January* 4, 1831.

"You are now a man possessed of as much leisure as you are ever likely to possess. What think you of laying in materials for a Doctrinal and practical History of Religion in England, in different classes of society, and of males and females, from the time of the Reformation to the present time or perhaps to 1760. It was once my wish to write such a work, but the state of my eyes long ago rendered it impracticable. The sources from whence the particulars for the work must be derived are chiefly Lives and Memoirs. Numbers of these have been published of late years, and the object is one which would give opportunities for exercising sagacity, as well as candour. There is this also of good in it that, *nullus dies sine lineâ*, you might be continually finding some fresh fact or hint, which would afterwards be capable of being turned to good account. The Annual Registers and the different magazines and reviews would be rich mines of raw material. Do meditate on these suggestions. How very strong has dear Henry become both in his opinions and his language! Really if he were to go into the law, which Robert seems to think not improbable, there would be considerable danger of his getting into quarrels which might draw on him challenges, the more probably because people might suppose from his parentage, &c., that he most likely would not answer a call to the field. I must say that the becoming exempt, even in the world's estimate, from the obligation to challenge or being challenged may be no unfair principle of preference of an ecclesiastical profession to any other. The subject of duelling is one which I never saw well treated; a very worthy and sensible man, a Scotchman who was shipwrecked in Madagascar, I forget his name (was it Duncan?) sent me one, his own writing, but I thought it *naught*. And now my very dear boy farewell."

Wilberforce writes to Mrs. Samuel Wilberforce the day after his daughter Elizabeth's marriage.

Mr. Wilberforce to Mrs. Samuel Wilberforce.

"HIGHWOOD HILL,
"*January* 12, 1831.

"MY DEAR EMILY,—We had a delightful day yesterday for our ceremony, and after the indissoluble knot had been tied in due form, the parties drove off about 12 o'clock to spend a few days at Mr. Stephen's favourite residence of Healthy Hill, as he terms it, Missenden. I really augur well of this connection, having strong reasons for believing Mr. James to be a truly aimable as well as pious man, and my dear Lizzy is really well fitted for the office of a parson's aider and comforter. It has given me no little pleasure to have been assured by Mr. Dupré, the curate of the parish, that she has been truly useful to the poor cottagers around us. His expression was, 'She has done more good than she knows of.' This event, combined with the close of another year and the anniversary of my own dear wife's birthday, has called forth in me a lively sense of the goodness of that gracious Being who has dealt so bountifully with me during a long succession of years. Dr. Warren, in 1788, as I was reminded when at Brighstone, declared that for want of stamina there would be an end of my feeble frame in two or three weeks, and then I was a bachelor. After this, near ten years after, I became a husband, and now I have assured me full grown descendants, and an offset in my Elizabeth. I have been receiving many congratulations from being perhaps the only living father of three first-class men, one of them a double first and the two others in the second also. Above all their literary acquirements I value their having, as I verily believe, passed through the fiery trial of an university, for such I honestly account it, without injury. And it gives me no little pleasure (as I think I have before assured you), to add that I ascribe this in part to the instrumentality of a certain young lady, who was a sort of guardian angel hovering around him in fancy and exerting a benign influence over the sensibility and tenderness of his lively spirit. Farewell, my dear Emily.

"Believe me, begging a kiss to baby,

"Ever affectionately yours,

"W. WILBERFORCE."

Mr. Wilberforce to the Rev. Samuel Wilberforce.
"*February* 8, 1831.

"My dear Samuel,—Pray both for your mother and for poor William that they may be delivered from μέριμνα. The former, alas! lies awake for hours in the morning, and cannot banish from her mind the carking cares that haunt and worry her. We profess to believe in the efficacy of prayer. Let us prove the truth of our profession by at least not acquiescing, without resistance, in such assailments. It is more from natural temperament than from any higher attainment that I am not the prey of these corrosions. Something may be ascribed to the habit of controlling my thoughts which I acquired when in public life. . . . You might, I believe, have shone in political life; but you have chosen the better part. And if you can think so now when in your younger blood, much more will you become sensible of it by and by when you look back, if God should so permit, on a long retrospect, studded with records of the Divine blessing on your ministerial exertions. Kindest remembrances to dear Emily, and a kiss to little Emily, and the blessing of your affectionate father,

"W. Wilberforce."

"Highwood Hill,
"*March* 4, 1831.

"I will frankly confess to you that I almost tremble

for the consequences of Lord Russell's plan of Reform if it should be carried. I wish the qualification had been higher. The addition to the County Representation lessens the danger. Much in the judgments we form on such practical questions depends on our period of life. I find myself now at seventy-one and a half far more timid and more indisposed to great changes, and less inclined to promise myself great benefit from political plans. I own I scarcely can expect the plan to succeed, especially in the House of Lords. We understand your invitation to be for July and August. But I foretell you plainly you shall not regularly walk with me, or break off any habits which can in any degree interfere with duty. We have not yet settled our plans. Indeed, they may greatly depend on the convenience of our friends. I well remember the Dean of Carlisle used to say when invitations multiplied, 'Do you think that if you wanted a dinner there would be so many disposed to give you one?' We are now about to put this to the proof. I own now that it comes to the point I am a little disposed to exclaim, 'O happy hills! O pleasing shades!' &c. But I should be ashamed were I to have any other prevailing feeling than thankfulness. I feel most the separation from my books. However, *sursum corda*."

Wilberforce writes to his friend Babington on Lord Russell's propositions :—

Mr. Wilberforce to Mr. Babington.

"HIGHWOOD HILL,
"*March* 14, 1831.

"MY DEAR TOM,—I fear you will be again disposed to accuse me of treating you with neglect (not, I hope, with unkindness) in suffering week after week to pass away without returning answers to your kind letters. I have really had as much necessary writing on my hands, as even when I was member for Yorkshire. But I cannot bear to think that you are, day after day, looking out for my handwriting (as you are opening your daily packets), and looking out in vain. There have been many topics, I assure you, on which I should have been glad to communicate with you had I been able. I know not how you have felt, but I must say I felt glad by the consciousness that I was not now in a situation to be compelled to approach, and act upon, the important question of Lord John Russell's proposition. On the whole, I think I should have been favourable to it; chiefly, or rather most confidently, from trusting that we shall do away with much vice and much bribery which now prevail. I am persuaded also that the change will be for the benefit, and greatly so, of our poor West India clients. I should like to know your sentiments on the plan."

Mr. Wilberforce to the Rev. Samuel Wilberforce.
"*April* 8, 1831.

"And now, my dear Samuel, we have commenced our wanderings. I write from Daniel Wilson's, who treats us with the utmost kindness."

From this time Wilberforce had no house of his own, but spent the remaining years of his life with his sons and with his friends. In his own language, he "became a wanderer without any certain dwelling-place."

"KENSINGTON GORE,
"*April* 20*th*.

"It must be three weeks or more since Lord Brougham, when on the woolsack, called Stephen,[1] then attending the House of Lords, quasi master (two of their description you perhaps know are required to be always present; they take down their Lordships' Bills to the House of Commons), and after expressing in very strong language his concern at having heard such an account as had reached him of the state of my finances, and more particularly of its being necessary for me to quit my own house, and become a wanderer without any certain dwelling-place, he stated that he had lately heard of my having sons and a son-in-law in the Church, and that he should be most happy to do what he could for them. Lord Milton afterwards, as I understand

[1] Mr. Wilberforce's brother-in-law.

from Dan Sykes, expressed to Lord Brougham some kind intentions towards me, and more especially that he waived a claim or an application he had been making for the living of Rawmarsh, as soon as he learned that Lord Brougham had destined it to me. Robert would not accept any living which would not afford me a suitable residence."

"*April* 23, 1831.

"You cannot conceive how little time I appear to have at my own command while passing our lives in this vagarious mode, which, however, calls forth emotions of gratitude to the Giver of all good, who has raised up for me so many and so kind friends. I ought not to forget, while a Gracious Providence has granted me a good name which is better than great riches, that many public men as upright as myself have been the victims of calumny. I myself indeed have had its envenomed shafts at times directed against me. But on the whole few men have suffered from them so little as myself."

"BATH, *October* 19, 1831.

"I am but poorly, and I am bothered (a vulgar phrase, but having been used in the House of Lords I may condescend to adopt it) with incessant visitors. There is a person come over to this country from the United States, of the Society of Quakers, for the excellent purpose of obtaining popularity and support for a society which has been in being for nine or ten years—the American Colonisation Society. I could not but assent to his proposal to pay me a visit at this place. The time was when such a visitor would have been no encumbrance to me. But now that he takes me in hand when I am already tired by others, (though it is only justice to him to say no one can be less intrusive or more obliging than he is), I do sink under it. My dear Samuel, it is one of the bad consequences of the plan you prescribed that I exhibit myself to you in the state of mind in which I am at the moment, though I should not otherwise have selected it for that purpose.

"*Friday*, 12 *o'clock, October* 21*st.*

"Our American friend has left us this morning But, alas! he has requested me to write in his album. What a vile system is the album system! No, I do not, I cannot think so, though I am somewhat ruffled by being called on for my contingent, when I have little or no supplies left to furnish it."

Wilberforce goes on to express his gratitude for the safety of his daughter Elizabeth (Mrs. James), who had been confined of a daughter.

"The mere circumstance that a new immortal being is produced and committed to our keeping is a consideration of extreme moment. Though I own it sometimes tends to produce emotions of a saddening character, to consider into what a world our new grandchild has entered, what stormy seas she will have to navigate. I will enclose an interesting passage I have received from Tom Babington, giving an account of Dr. Chalmer's speculations.

"I own I am sadly alarmed for the Church. There is such a combination of noxious elements fermenting together, that I am ready to exclaim, 'There is death in the pot,' and there will be, I fear, no Elisha granted to us to render the mess harmless. But yet I am encouraged to hope that the same gracious and longsuffering Being who would have spared Sodom for ten, and Jerusalem even for one righteous man's sake, may spare us to the prayers of the many who do, I trust, sincerely sigh and cry in behalf of our proud, ungrateful land. Yet, again, when I consider what light we have enjoyed, what mercies we have received, and how self-sufficient and ungrateful we have been, I am again tempted to despond. I wish I could be a less unprofitable servant. Yet I must remember Milton's sonnet, 'They also serve who only stand and wait.' Let us all be found in our several stations doing therein the Lord's work diligently and zealously. What do you think of Shuttleworth's new translation of St. Paul's Epistles? I have borrowed but not yet read them. Affectionate remembrances to dear Emily, and a kiss to sweet baby."

"BLAIZE CASTLE,[1]
"*October* 31, 1831.

"You will hear what dreadful work has been going on at Bristol for the last eight and forty hours. Sir Charles Wetherell[2] escaped from the fury of the mob by first hiding himself in some upper room in the Mansion House and then passing, disguised in a sack jacket, from the roof of the Mansion House to that of another house, whence he got to a distant part of the town, and in a chaise and four returned in all haste, (they say) to London. He was, as Recorder, to have opened the Commission and tried all the prisoners to-day. However, the latter are now all at work again in their accustomed callings. Not a single gaol, I am assured, is left undestroyed. The Bishop's Palace, (and Deanery too I am told), burnt to the ground. The Custom House ditto, Mansion House ditto. Poor Pinney, the Mayor, I was assured, behaved on Saturday with great presence of mind. The populace, however, got into the Mansion House before the corporation went to dinner; so all the

[1] The seat of J. S. Harford, Esq.
[2] Lord Grey's Reform Bill had amongst its most vehement opponents Sir C. Wetherell, Recorder of Bristol. On his arrival in that city the riots began there by an attack upon his carriage, after which "Bristol was the theatre of the most disgraceful outrages that have been perpetrated in this country since the riots of London, 1780." (*An. Reg.* 1831.)

good things regaled the ὁι πολλοι. Strange to say, (just as in the London riots), people were allowed to walk the streets in peace, and last night half the people in the square were looking on at the depredations committing by the other half. Well-dressed ladies walked about great part of the night staring as at a raree show. The redness of the sky from the conflagration was quite a dreadful sight to us in the distance. It is said they are endeavouring to organise a force for the defence of the city. It is very strange that this has been so long delayed. I'm assured pillage has latterly been the grand object. The deputation, I am told, were followed by a cart, in which, as they went along, they stowed the plunder. I have not said it to your mother, for fear of her becoming still more nervous,[1] (which need not be), by her finding me entertaining such cogitations, but if I perceive any grumblings of the volcano at Bath, before the lava bursts forth I shall hurry your mother to a certain quiet parsonage—though, alas! I cannot but fear for the Church in these days."

"BLAIZE CASTLE, *November* 2.

"The Bristol riots, though in some particulars

---

[1] Mrs. Wilberforce writes to her son Samuel: "Shall I send you the deeds, &c., to take care of for the family, and the plate to bury in your garden? I think you will be safe in the Isle of Wight. Do not let my fears be mentioned; they say we should all appear brave and bold."

the accounts were as usual exaggerated, were quite horrible, and the *great* events as reported. But a striking instance was afforded how easily perpetrations, if I may use the word, the most horrible may be at once arrested by determined opposition. On Monday morning early the mobs were parading about without resistance. But on that morning the troops, a small body of dragoons, charged them repeatedly at full speed, and not sparing either the momentum or the sharpness of their swords, no attempt at making a head afterwards appeared. Afterwards the day was properly employed in appointing a great number of special constables and other civil force, and every night, as well as day, since has passed in perfect quiet. A great part of the plunder has been recovered, and numbers of criminals have been seized — some of them sent to a gaol about seven miles off; and happily the condemned cells have escaped the fury of the mob, and have afforded a stronghold for keeping the prisoners. I need not tell you in what a ferment the mind of our host was thrown, indeed with great reason. He had been threatened with a visit at this place, and the best pictures were stowed away in safe custody. I am persuaded it has become indispensably necessary to form in all our great cities and neighbourhoods a civil police, properly armed and drilled. And thus, as usual, out of evil good may arise."

"BATH, *November* 13, 1831.

"I think you know Mr. Pearse of this place, an excellent and very agreeable man, and master of the Grammar School at this place, a large and flourishing one. He is a very musical man, an intimate and long attached friend of Dr. Crotch. I will consult him about your organ. I believe I told you that I scarcely ever remember finding my time so little equal to the claims on it as at this place, though were I asked 'What are you doing?' I should, alas! say 'Nothing'; and even, 'What have you to do?' still the same reply, 'Nothing' I have one occupation of an interesting and in some degree of an embarrassing nature. Soon after our arrival, I learnt that the only other inmate of our house was a gentleman who had been confined to his sofa for many months from the effects of a rheumatic fever. He had no friends with him, only a family servant who attended on him. Naturally feeling for the poor man, he and ourselves being the only inmates, I sent a message to him to say that, if agreeable, I should be happy to wait on him for a few minutes. He returned an assenting and courteous reply. Accordingly I called, and found a very civil and well-behaved man. I found that he had been fond of game, and had expressed his regret that he could not purchase it (this was his servant's report). Accordingly I sent him some now and then. I soon afterwards was told that he was a Roman Catholic. He is by profession a lawyer at Pontypool. I have since had several conversations with him, and find him a decided Roman Catholic, but a man apparently of great candour and moderation. I was not surprised to find him strongly prejudiced against Blanco White.[1] 'Oh,' he cried, 'I assure you, sir, that book is full of the grossest falsehood.' But I was a good deal surprised to receive from him an assurance that he had been reading with great pleasure in a book of my writing; and I found, to my surprise, that quite unknown to me Kendal had lent him the book. I durst not have done it, but the event has taught me that we may sometimes be too timid or delicate. Can you suggest any mode of dealing with my fellow lodger? Hitherto I have gone on the plan of cultivating his favourable opinion by general kindness, sending him game,

[1] T. Blanco White, a Spaniard by birth, left the Church of Rome and joined the Church of England, and also became a naturalised Englishman. He was closely connected with the Oxford movement, but lapsed into Socinianism. He died in 1841.

&c., and endeavouring to press on him the most important doctrines of true Christianity and of showing where the case is really so, that he may embrace those doctrines and still continue a good Roman Catholic. There is in the *Christian Observer* for September last a critique on Dr. Whately's sermons by the Bishop of Chichester. He is said, in the outset, to have stated in a pamphlet on the Bible Society controversy, that the only books in the Scriptures which were fit or useful for general circulation were Genesis, Exodus, Job, Psalms, Proverbs, I think Isaiah, but am not sure, the four Gospels, Acts, 1st Timothy, 1st Peter, 1st John and Jude; all the rest likely to do more harm than good."

"BATH, *December* 6, 1831.

"I am unaffectedly sorry for having been apparently so dilatory in complying with your request for hymns and tunes. I use the word *apparently*, because to any charge of suffering any opportunity of executing the commission to pass by unimproved, I may boldly plead not guilty. There never, surely, was such a place as this for the frittering away of time. Two visits before breakfast to the Pump Room, and two again from 2 to $3\frac{1}{4}$ o'clock in the afternoon, make such a chasm in the day, that little before dinner (about $4\frac{3}{4}$) is left for any rational occupation.

Then not being able, for many reasons, to receive company at dinner, we often invite friends to breakfast, and as we cannot begin the meal till 10½ at the soonest, we seldom have a clear room till after 12. Sometimes morning callers come in before the breakfasters are gone (as has been the case this morning, when my old friend Bankes has entered, taking Bath in his way from his son in North Wales into Dorsetshire). You owe this account of expenditure of my time to my feeling quite uncomfortable, from the idea of neglecting a commission you wished to consign to me for prompt execution. I will put down in any letter I may write to you any hymns and hymn tunes which I like ('Happy the heart where graces reign,' Lock tune), and you may add together the *disjecta membra* into one list. But I have not hymn-books here except G. Noel's. At Highwood I have a considerable number. Your poor mother is worried to pieces by company and business. I am fully persuaded, my dear Samuel, that you wish to lighten the pressure on me as much as possible, and on the other hand I doubt not you give me full credit for wishing to make you as comfortable as I can, and I really hope I shall be able to go on allowing my children what is necessary for their comfort."

"*January* 19, 1832.

"St. John says, you will remember, 'I have no greater joy than to know that my children walk in the truth.' This he could declare concerning his figurative children. And well, therefore, ought we to be able, at least, to desire to feel similar sensations on witnessing the graces of our true, real children. And I am in a situation to feel this with peculiar force. Indeed, I hope I can say with truth that the more frequent, more continued and closer opportunities of witnessing your conscientious and diligent discharge of your pastoral duties—opportunities which I probably should not have enjoyed in the same degree had I still a residence of my own—more than compensate all I suffer from the want of a proper home. Indeed, there are but two particulars that I at all feel, *i.e.*, the absence of my books, and the not being able to practise hospitality; though that is rather a vulgar word for expressing my meaning, which is, the pleasure of receiving those we love under our own roof, joining with them morning and night in family prayers, shaking hands with them, and interchanging continual intercourse of mutual affection. Well, the time is short, even for those who are far less advanced than myself in the journey of life."

"BATH, *June* 14, 1832.

"I forget whether you know the Dean of Winchester[1] or not. We have many a discussion together, and I now and then stroke his plumage the wrong way to make him set up his bristles. He holds the great degeneracy of these times. I, on the contrary, declared to him that, though I acknowledged the more open prevalence of profaneness, and of all the vices which grow out of insubordination, yet that there had been also a marked and a great increase of religion within the last forty years. And as a proof I assigned the numerous editions of almost all the publications of family prayers, beginning with the Rector of St. Botolph's (Bishop of London's)."

"*July* 12, 1832.

"Though I do not like to mention it to your mother, I feel myself becoming more and more stupid and inefficient. I think it is chiefly a bodily disease, at least there, I hope, is the root of the disease. I am so languid after breakfast that, if I am read to, I infallibly subside into a drowsiness, which, if not resisted by my getting up and walking, or taking for a few minutes the book Joseph may be reading to me, gradually slides into a state of complete stupor. Yet it is down-

---

[1] Dr. Thomas Rennell: he was appointed in 1805, and was succeeded in 1840 by Dr. Garnier.

right shocking in me to use language which may at all subject me justly to the imputation of repining. And to be just to myself, I do not think I am fairly chargeable with that fault. I hope that which might at first sight seem to have somewhat of that appearance is rather the compunctious visitings of my better part grieving over my utter uselessness. I do not like to give expression to these distressing risings, because I may not unreasonably appear to be calling for friendly assurances in return of my having been an active labourer. Yet when I am pouring forth the effusions of my heart to a child to whom I may open myself with the freedom I may justly practise towards you, I do not like to keep in reserve my real feelings. My memory is continually giving me fresh proofs of its decaying at an accelerated rate of progress. But I will not harass your affectionate feelings; and however I may lament my unprofitableness, and at times really feel depressed by it, yet my natural cheerfulness of temper produces in my exterior such an appearance of good spirits that I might be supposed by my daily associates to be living in an atmosphere of unclouded comfort. So you need not be distressing yourself on my account."

The rest of this letter shows that Wilberforce had asked the advice of Samuel as to the wisdom of engaging a Roman Catholic tutor for his grandson "dear little William."[1] Samuel's answer was couched in decisive terms against this step. Wilberforce, however, was reconciled to the idea by the knowledge that "dear little William's mother will be always on the spot, always on her guard, watchful and ready to detect and proceed against any attempt whatever which might be made to bias William's mind into undervaluing the importance of the difference between the Roman Catholic and the Protestant system, or still more to infuse into his pupil's mind any prejudices against our principles or personages, or any palliations of the Popish tenets."

In the concluding year of Wilberforce's life, though he complains of "becoming more and more stupid and inefficient," the feelings and thoughts which animated his life appear in full vigour. His watchful love for his children, his hospitality, the steady, faithful looking forward to the life everlasting—all are there. Nor, until he has made one more effort to secure the freedom of the slaves, does the weary, diligent hand finally "lay down the pen."

"*December* 18, 1832.

"Although we should use great modesty in speculating on the invisible and eternal world, yet we may reasonably presume from intimations

[1] Only son of Wilberforce's eldest son William.

conveyed to us in the Holy Scriptures, and from inferences which they fairly suggest, that we shall retain of our earthly character and feelings in that which is not sinful, and therefore we may expect (this, I think, is very clear), to know each other, and to think and talk over the various circumstances of our lives, our several hopes and fears and plans and speculations; and you and I, if it please God, may talk over the incidents of our respective lives, and connected with them, those of our nearest and dearest relatives. And, then, probably we shall be enabled to understand the causes of various events which at the time had appeared mysterious."

"*December* 28, 1832.

"I should wish to suggest to you an idea that arises from a passage in a letter from William Smith.[1] The idea is that it might have a very good effect, for any of my reverend children to be known to manifest their zeal in the great cause of West Indian emancipation, and slaves' improvement. And as I am on that topic let me tell you, I need not say with how much pleasure, that I really believe we are now going on admirably. The slaves will, I trust, be immediately placed under the government of the same laws as other

---

[1] "My most faithful friend, William Smith" ("Life of Wilberforce," vol. iii. p. 536).

members of the community, instead of being under the arbitrary commands of their masters, and (perhaps after a year) they will be still more completely emancipated. I was truly glad to find in the evidence taken before the House of Commons' Committee (which the indefatigable Zachary[1] is analysing), highly honourable testimony to our friend's (Wildman's) treatment of his slaves. But I ought not to conceal from you the connection in which W. Smith's suggestion of the great benefit that would result from my sons taking a forward part in befriending the attempts that would be made to stir up a petitioning spirit in support of our cause, (for he informed me that efforts for that purpose would be made). He stated that it had been observed almost everywhere that the clergy had been shamefully lukewarm in our cause; and of course this, which I fear cannot be denied, has been used in many instances for the injury of the Church. You and I see plainly how this has happened: that the most active supporters of our cause have too often been democrats, and radicals, with whom the regular clergy could not bring themselves to associate. Yet even when subjected to such a painful alternative, to unite with them, or to suffer the interests of justice and humanity, and latterly of religion too, to be in

[1] Macaulay.

question without receiving any support from them, or to do violence to, I will not say their prejudices, but their natural repugnance to appearing to have anything of a fellow-feeling with men who are commonly fomenting vicious principles and propositions of all sorts; when placed, I say, in such distressing circumstances, they should remember that their coming forward, in accordance with those with whom they agree in no other particular, will give additional weight to their exertions, and prove still more clearly how strongly they feel the cause of God, and the well-being of man to be implicated, when they can consent to take part with those to whom in general they have been opposed most strongly. The conduct of the Jamaica people towards the missionaries has shown of late, more clearly than ever before, that the spiritual interests of the slaves, no less than their civil rights, are at stake. In such a case as this, it is not without pain and almost shame that I urge any argument grounded on the interests of the clergy; and yet it would be wrong to keep considerations of this sort altogether out of sight, because one sees how malignantly and injuriously to the cause of religion the apathy of the clergy may, and will, be used, to the discredit of the Church, and its most attached adherents. It is not a little vexatious to find people so ignorant, as too many are, concerning the real state of the slaves, notwithstanding all the pains that have been taken to enlighten them. Stephen's book in particular has, I fear, been very little read. When we were at Lord Bathurst's I saw plainly that the speeches of a Mr. Borthwick, who had been going about giving lectures in favour of the West Indians, had made a great impression on Lady Georgiana. But I must lay down my pen."

The Gresham Press,
UNWIN BROTHERS
WOKING AND LONDON.

Second Edition. *With Portraits, cloth, price* **12s.**

THE YEAR AFTER THE ARMADA,

And other Historical Studies.

BY

MARTIN A. S. HUME.

Press Notices.

THE TIMES—
"Major Hume tells the story in full detail and with great spirit. . . . Very interesting."

THE DAILY TELEGRAPH, W. L. COURTNEY in—
"Major Hume has thrown the most curious and valuable light on the Armada period. Full of delightful sketches of men and things."

THE DAILY CHRONICLE—
"Mr. Hume has already established his reputation as an authority on Anglo-Spanish relations in the Elizabethan age. . . . A most fascinating picture. . . We are glad to recommend Mr. Hume's interesting volume, and we trust he will still further extend his researches into Spanish life."

THE MORNING POST—
"A work which adds many a fresh page to English, and, one may say to European history. . . . From first to last the volume is excellent reading, while the entertaining style in which the matter is presented and the undeniable authority of the writer . . . render the book of special interest and permanent value."

COSMOPOLIS, ANDREW LANG in—
"Quite as good as a novel—and a good deal better, too. The book is so bright and vivid that readers with the common dislike of history may venture on its pages unafraid."

THE GLOBE—
"Major Hume furnishes us with much that is as instructive and valuable as it is readable."

PALL MALL GAZETTE—
"Mr. Hume has had luck and he deserves his luck. We hope he will give us some more of his 'chips' and clippings from the records of the past."

THE ATHENÆUM—
"'The evolution of the Spanish Armada' is an essay of the first importance. . . . 'The Coming of Philip the Prudent,' is a most interesting account of Philip's voyage, his arrival in England, and his marriage to the Queen."

PRESS NOTICES—*Continued.*

THE SPEAKER—
"Whatever Mr. Hume writes on the subject which he has made his own is sure to be good in substance and bright in style. Extremely interesting, and at once instructive and amusing."

THE NEW SATURDAY—
"Very delightful.... Everything he has to tell is worth hearing, and to listen is easy by reason of the good telling.... We could go on indefinitely dipping thus into Mr. Hume's pleasant pages, but enough has been said, we trust, to induce readers to obtain the book for themselves, and it is to be hoped that the author will continue to give us the fruit of his researches."

THE TABLET—
"The volume presents much careful and critical research, and the results are offered in a spirit of impartiality and historical detachment of which we gladly make acknowledgment."

NOTES AND QUERIES—
"Thanks to the researches Major Hume is making, the history of Tudor times has to be entirely rewritten.... The whole is well-written, interesting, luminous, and valuable. The book has genuine historical value."

THE SHEFFIELD INDEPENDENT—
"A bright and unusual book."

THE LIVERPOOL DAILY POST—
"No aphorism so apologetic is needed to recommend or preface a book by Major Hume, who has gathered from unexplored quarters great stores of historic lore, and who has a pleasant gift of bright expression which makes interesting, even to the casual reader, his essays and studies."

GLASGOW HERALD—
"Most interesting reading. It is certain to attract the attention of students of history, and it may be confidently commended to all who can enjoy a vivacious narrative of long past events, or a realistic description of vanished manners."

MANCHESTER CITY NEWS—
"The story is told with great spirit by Major Hume in a volume full of novelty and varied interest."

THE OBSERVER—
"Readers of these historical studies will find a great deal that is good, new, and interesting. We cordially recommend them to our readers."

THE SPECTATOR—
"Mr. Hume will add very greatly to the reputation as a serious but not dryasdustish or pedagogic historical investigator which he obtained by his 'Courtships of Queen Elizabeth' ... He has a remarkable faculty for producing life-like portraits of men who are at once strong and scoundrelly."

PUBLISHERS' CIRCULAR—
"Seldom have we come across such interesting and well-written historical essays. The book is brightly written and handsomely produced."

LONDON :
T. FISHER UNWIN, PATERNOSTER SQUARE, E.C.

THE COURTSHIPS OF QUEEN ELIZABETH:

A HISTORY OF THE VARIOUS NEGOTIATIONS FOR HER MARRIAGE.

By Martin A. S. Hume.

Fourth Edition, with portraits. Cloth, 12s.

"A clear and very interesting account. An excellent book."—*The Times*.

"We would counsel a perusal of that very remarkable volume, 'The Courtships of Queen Elizabeth,' which, besides being in the highest degree entertaining, furnishes utterly new views of the spacious times of great Elizabeth."—*The Daily Telegraph* (Leading Article).

"A delightful book."—*The Daily Telegraph* (Review).

"Without a perusal of Mr. Hume's most researchful and interesting volume, no one, no student even of Froude can claim to have thoroughly grasped the character and aims of our good Queen Bess."—*The Daily Chronicle*.

"Mr. Hume, who is the learned editor of the Calendar of Spanish State Papers issued by the Record Office, has gone to the fountain-head. A connected and consistent—though assuredly a most extraordinary story. A fascinating picture."—*Standard* (Leader).

"Mr. Hume has performed his task admirably. In his hands the story of a unique series of farcical courtships becomes a luminous study in sixteenth century international diplomacy."—*The Daily News*.

"A luminous and fascinating narrative. Mr. Hume's masterly and impartial narrative. It is undeniably an important addition to the history of the Elizabethan period, and it will rank as the foremost authority on the most interesting aspect of the character of the Tudor Queen."—*Pall Mall Gazette*.

"Among the historians of the later Victorian era Mr. Hume will take high rank. His contributions to our knowledge of Elizabethan times are the result of attainments which no other writer can claim to possess. He is to be congratulated on producing a work with which no student can afford to dispense if desirous of understanding the character of Elizabeth, and which no other living Englishman could have produced."—*The Observer*.

THE COURTSHIPS OF QUEEN ELIZABETH (continued).

"Mr. Hume is a serious authority with far too great a keenness for facts to be a partisan. One might make dozens of pointed extracts, but the book is distinctly one to be read by those who care for past manners."—*Daily Courier*.

"Mr. Hume tells an interesting tale with enviable clearness and felicity of language. He may claim to have made a valuable addition to our knowledge of one of the greatest of our national benefactors."—*The Echo*.

"Eminently thorough and lucid, and throws fresh light on what has long been one of the most perplexing as it will ever be the most amusing chapter in the English annals."—*The Glasgow Herald*.

"The volume is based on authentic State papers . . . explored with great pains and marvellous industry."—*Dublin Daily Telegraph*.

"A careful and learned piece of work."—*Manchester Guardian*.

"A serious and able work."—*Spectator*.

"This volume is a splendid contribution to English history."—*The Birmingham Gazette*.

"The story is altogether a very remarkable one, and is now told for the first time with fulness and accuracy. Students of English and European history during the critical sixteenth century period cannot afford to overlook this strikingly interesting volume."—*The Freeman*.

"A very curious and important chapter in English history . . . throws a flood of light on the character and methods of the Queen."—*The Tablet*.

"Written in a charmingly clear literary style, and the solid character of its contents should recommend it to serious readers."—*Aberdeen Free Press*.

"Extremely interesting. The author is to be congratulated on having written a most entertaining record."—*The Daily Graphic*.

"It has the interest of a novel. This engrossing history of the various negotiations for the Queen's marriage."—*The Sketch*.

LONDON:
T. FISHER UNWIN, PATERNOSTER SQUARE, E.C.

fe and Letters of Mr. Endymion Porter:
Sometime Gentleman
of the Bedchamber
to King Charles
the First

By Dorothea Townshend

With Portraits

[In Preparation

LONDON: T. FISHER UNWIN

CPSIA information can be obtained at www.ICGtesting.com
Printed in the USA
LVOW091933130213

319976LV00007B/362/P